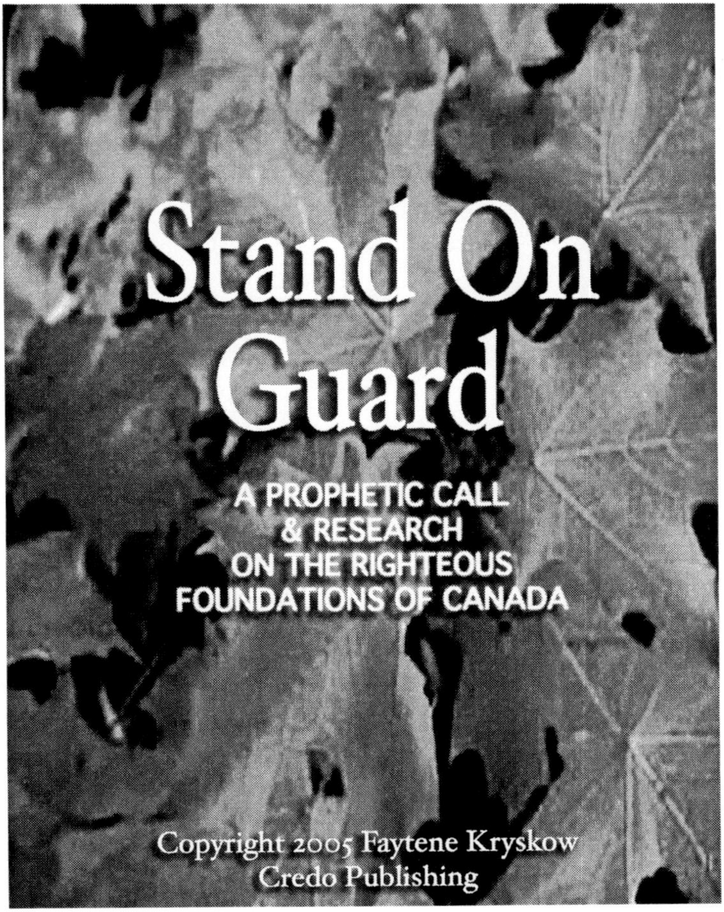
Stand On
Guard
A PROPHETIC CALL
& RESEARCH
ON THE RIGHTEOUS
FOUNDATIONS OF CANADA
Copyright 2005 Faytene Kryskow
Credo Publishing

ISBN 0-9737510-0-2

6717 Wales St., Vancouver, BC, Canada, V5S 2R7.
Printed in Canada.
Independently published with Credo Publishing.

FIN 03 02 06

"He shall have dominion also from sea to sea,
And from the River to the ends of the earth.
Those who dwell in the wilderness will bow before Him,
And His enemies will lick the dust...
Yes, all kings shall fall down before Him;
All nations shall serve Him.
For He will deliver the needy when he cries,
The poor also, and him who has no helper."
(Psalm 72: 8, 11-12)

This book is dedicated to
"He" who is spoken of in Psalm 72:8,
Jesus Christ: King of the Nations,
&
to a generation yet unborn.

Special Acknowledgement To:

Michael Clarke for his exceptional research compilation
in Canada: Portraits of the Faith.
Portions of Chapters 1 and 2 have been
significantly enriched by this compilation.

Other personal thanks and special
acknowledgements are listed following the Index.

RECOMMENDATIONS

"I am convinced that untold numbers of Canadians (and others) will be inspired as they discover that much of Canada's untold history is steeped in the lives of people of faith. This book clearly demonstrates that Canada's institutions are resting on pillars of principle built by Canadians who were unassuming and unswerving in living out their faith in the public square."

Stockwell Day, M.P.
Official Opposition Foreign Affairs Critic
Okanagan-Coquihalla, B.C., Canada

"I am absolutely delighted that Faytene Kryskow has written *Stand On Guard*. This is the first in-depth account I am aware of that clearly accounts for the uniqueness of Canada in its calling and in its purpose as a nation...I believe Faytene has given us the blueprint that testifies to Canada's spiritual DNA! Take your Bible, some paper and a pen – and prepare to undertake a journey that enables the reader to see through the grid of the Holy Spirit that the destiny of a nation is found in the Hands of the Living God Himself!"

Rev. Dr. Alistair P. Petrie
Author and Director of Partnership Ministries
Kelowna, B.C., Canada

"Faytene has a heart for her generation and a heart for this nation. I believe this book flows from the depths of her heart, and will inspire and influence many other young and gifted leaders like her."

David Demian
Director of Watchmen for the Nations
Vancouver, B.C., Canada

"Faytene is a brilliant young writer, communicator and emerging historian with a unique researching capacity to unlock Canada's history through a prophetic perspective that makes her work highly relevant at this time. Her writing is captivating, rich in content, and filled with a spiritual passion for the redemptive destiny of Canada to be realized."

Pastor Len Zoeteman
Full Gospel Church
Calgary, Alberta, Canada

"Faytene Kryskow has captured the passion of the LORD for this critical moment in Canadian history. A generation of 'Dread Champions' are being raised up who just like David's mighty men will stand in the field of this glorious nation to secure it for the King. Both hope and faith will rise in your heart and stir you to action as you read this prophetic trumpet call."

Patricia King
Christian Services Association
and Founder/Overseer of Extreme Prophetic
Kelowna, B.C., Canada

"*Stand On Guard* is an invaluable tool for any Christian who wants to understand the spiritual foundations of the nation of Canada. It is a call to prayer and a call to examine the spiritual foundations that made our country unique amongst the nations of the world. It is a must read for those who seek to understand Canada and Canadians."

Stacey Campbell
Revival Now Ministries
and Founder/Overseer of the Canadian Prophetic Council
Kelowna, B.C., Canada

"Faytene Kryskow is blowing the trumpet for this generation. This is a clear call to rise up in the godly heritage of Canada, pick up the baton from our forefathers, and become the generation that will fulfill the dream of the LORD for our nation!"

Alain Caron
Pastor of Le Chemin
Senior Leader with Watchmen for the Nations
Ottawa, Ontario, Canada

8

"I would like to recommend that leaders take the time to read this book. Especially for those that have a heart for this nation of Canada. This book is enlightening and refreshing. God is raising up this generation and they carry a word that needs to be heard. Faytene has reminded us that we need to honor Canada's historical roots. As an Inuit person who has observed the development of this country, it is at the verge of losing its identity and this book reminds Canadians of their righteous roots. May the LORD bless you as you read this book."

James T. Arreak
Senior Pastor of Iqaluit Christian Fellowship
Inuit Leader

"The documents presented in *Stand On Guard* have provided irrefutable evidences for the people of God with legal rights to reclaim the nation and to help fulfill the dream of the LORD for Canada. Let those who have ears to hear what the Holy Spirit is saying to the Church - rise up quickly to answer the prophetic call of the generation."

Pastor Gideon Chiu
Apostolic Leader of Church of Zion
Vancouver, B.C., Canada

"This book is filled with passion and great information as Faytene calls Christians to stand for righteousness and to pray for Canada. One cannot help but feel proud of our forefathers and yet challenged to know that what they contended for has not yet been realized in our nation. Faytene's heart is for us to capture this same passion of our forefathers that we will see Canada's destiny fulfilled."

Rob and Fran Parker
Founders/Overseers of the National House of Prayer
Ottawa, Ontario, Canada

"I have had the privilege of knowing Faytene for several years, and it has been a joy to watch the increasing strength of anointing, giftings and maturity in her life. Her love for a nation, has led her to invest both time, research and passion, in calling for an awakening to greater awareness of the righteous foundations of Canada. Jeremiah 6:16 says, 'Stand in the ways and see, and ask for the ancient paths, where the good way is, and walk in it; and you will find rest for your souls.' I believe *Stand On Guard* will not only inspire, but challenge each of us, to return to the foundation of our roots, and earnestly seek the LORD in prayer, that, once again, righteousness and the Lordship of Jesus Christ, will be established in Canada."

Sheryl Lindberg
National President Aglow International of Canada
Bowmanville, Ontario, Canada

"*Stand On Guard*! What a resource! Faytene re-digs ancient wells and our generation drinks in abundance."

Danielle Strickland and Stephen Court
Founders/Overseers of Salvation Army 614
Vancouver, B.C., Canada

"Whether standing on the shorelines of the east or west coasts or upon the open, welcoming lands of our prairies, you can almost hear an echo which surpasses even the amazing natural beauty. Faytene has caught the sound of that echo of the faith of our fathers which is etched into this great land of Canada. She has found in our archives the footprints of faith, vision, and commitment to God's plan of destiny for this nation...which is really by His design a 'community of nations'. With this book we are reminded and comforted to know that this great land of the maple leaf is strategically positioned for eternal purposes of God. Everything which God has done is because of what God is going to do!"

Jack and Peggy Kennedy
Two Silver Trumpets Ministries
Brampton, Ontario, Canada

Drawing on the work of many historians, Faytene Kryskow has crafted a panoramic overview of how Canada's roots are set deeply in our pioneers' Biblical faith. And she has created what many previous historians had hinted at, but none had accomplished so clearly: a clarion call to "this generation" from the youngest to the oldest of us to petition God for fulfillment of His purposes in and for Canada, and for the power to fulfill our role in His plans for the world.

Ron Gray
National Leader
Christian Heritage Party of Canada

"I commend Faytene Kryskow and her book for her vision, compassion and heart for a restored Canada."

Rev. Ed Hird
St. Simons Anglican Church
North Vancouver, B.C., Canada

"*Stand on Guard* stirs me to step forward and participate in the reclaiming of our nation's spiritual inheritance. I believe you will be stirred to faith and Spirit-led action for the transformation of this nation when you read this book. Thanks Faytene for being a catalyst in all of this."

Pastor Calvin Weber
Westpointe Christian Centre
(Faytene Kryskow's home church)
Vancouver, B.C., Canada

TABLE OF CONTENTS

"In the middle of its streets, and on either side of the river,
was the tree of life, which bore twelve fruits,
each tree yielding its fruit every month.
The leaves of the tree were for the healing of the nations."
(Revelation 22:2)

PREFACE

Every generation and every nation has had **righteous radicals** for God. These were mighty men and women who laid down their lives to see righteousness established in their generation, and, in their nation. **Canada is no different.** Our history is full of heroes of the faith who forged rough terrain, braved harsh climates, persevered long voyages, endured brutal persecution and overcame intense spiritual warfare for the sake of the Kingdom of God in this land. These ones sacrificed to see the gospel of Jesus Christ advanced and His name honoured at various stages of the nation's growth. *Stand On Guard* is full of their stories and statements. However, more than a collection of research, this book is **a trumpet call** — a call to the current generation to rise up and do the same! It is a call **to bring into view, reestablish, and steward the righteous foundations** laid by generations past, and, it is a call to **reformation** of the unrighteous ideals and systems that have taken root in Canada. *Stand On Guard* reminds us of our inheritance as Canadians, so that, we will have added confidence to **"STAND"** in our generation and fight to see the dominion of Jesus Christ manifested in every arena of the nation. **What is our inheritance? It is a nation whose dominion was given to Jesus Christ at the foundation.** It is a nation full of the intense labours, and even the spilled blood, of those who were committed to establishing it in righteousness.

As those who confess Christ in the current generation, it is our mandate to ensure that not only are those foundations honoured but that they are fortified and built upon for the generations to come.

Should you have ever doubted that, as Canadians, we have a rich inheritance of righteousness I pray that this writing and compilation will convince you otherwise. Those who have gone before us repeatedly sacrificed to advance the Kingdom of God in this nation, and, repeatedly offered it up to the LORD. Each chapter of **Stand On Guard** presents research from a different portion of our history in which this commitment was made apparent.

The **PROPHETIC INTRODUCTION** chronicles a very personal, but corporately applicable, journey that the Holy Spirit has had me on since December 2003. This pilgrimage has been filled with moments of revelation and experiences that propelled me to write the book you are now holding. Sharing these personal moments of revelation with you, and the exhortations that stem from them, will set the stage for the research and give, what I believe is, a part of the framework for its application.

CHAPTERS 1 & 2 guide us through the experiences and heart intentions of many of the nation's first leaders. These missionaries, explorers, politicians, and the like held within their hearts a deep passion for God. They lit a torch that is extended to our generation to carry in this leg of history. **CHAPTER 3** (one of my favorites) gives powerful quotes from the nation's newspapers, from the East Coast to Ontario, during our first week as a unified nation (July 1867). These quotes are deeply inspiring and reveal the hopes, perspectives and dreams in the hearts of Canadians all across the land on the week that marks our nation's birth. I believe you will be encouraged and blessed by what you read from the archives of our very own newspapers! **CHAPTER 4** (another personal favorite) gathers lyrics from both the current national anthem and other versions sung across the nation over the years. Like the newspapers, they reveal a deep faith in the heart of the nation and give great glory to God. **CHAPTERS 5 & 6** look at Canada's name, flag, crest and Parliament buildings — most all of

18

which either reference the LORD with honour or point to our destiny, which was, ordained by Him. *CHAPTER 7* outlines prayers that have been prayed at the opening of House of Commons sessions since 1877, as well as, dialogue from the House of Commons debates regarding the establishment of these prayers. *CHAPTER 8* highlights sentiments from key national leaders regarding one of our most prominent struggles throughout history: relational tension between French and English speaking Canada. Finally, as a companion to the book, the *Musical Companion* (on CD) has recordings of three songs birthed in personal times of prayer for the nation. Each one was written as the LORD was working in my heart, imparting a deep burden for Canada.

The first song, *Confederation Song,* is composed of lyrics taken completely from what was in our nation's newspaper on Confederation Day 1867. This song was downloaded into my heart during a Watchmen for the Nations Leadership Gathering in Ottawa, March 2004, shortly after I had done the research for Chapter 3. As already mentioned, the words written in our newspapers are so powerful — I believe you will sense the anointing on them as you listen. I wrote Song #2, *Oh Canada,* years ago when the LORD first began to grip my heart for the nation and speak to me regarding our destiny to bring healing to the nations.[1] Finally, Song #3, *May I Have This Dance?,* was written for the 2003 cross-Canada La Danse Tour.[2] It is sung from an English-speaking Canadian perspective to French-speaking Canada, and, is a plea for the emergence of the type of unity that our forefathers intended for Confederation when they referred to it as a "Holy Matrimony" between the provinces involved.[3]

I have wept often, with a sovereign and deepening love for Canada, while writing and editing this book. With equal, or greater, intensity I pray that as you read it that it strikes a chord deep in your heart and leaves you forever changed. May *Stand On Guard* and the inheritance it presents impart an unshakable zeal within you for the manifestation of His glory in Canada. May this work, and others like it, propel our generation to radically arise with passion in our hearts, to lay down our lives, as our forefathers did, and labour relentlessly for His name's sake in Canada. **May both you, and I, be found on the front lines – FEARLESSLY FAITHFUL.**

---

[1] See pages 116 and 214 for more reference regarding Canada's destiny to bring healing to the nations.

[2] Visit www.watchmen.org for more information on the La Danse Tour of 2003.

[3] The direct reference to Confederation as a Holy Matrimony is found on page 247, other similar references were made in the nation's newspapers. These references can be found in Chapter 3.

Before we begin I would love to pray together.

Prayer:

Father, we thank You for those who have gone before us, for those who laid down their lives for this nation and who declared through word and deed at the foundation of Canada that You will have dominion from sea to sea! Thank You for the inheritance they have left for us, for the great sacrifice that they endured and for the strength and grace that You gave them. Now, Father, we pray You would empower us with great strength by Your Spirit to do the same, and more! Give us courage and give us undivided focus for Your glory. LORD we pray that You would speak to our hearts as we meditate on this righteous history, and, that You would fall upon us with Your Spirit. Mark us for Your purposes in this nation. Help us to see what You want us to see, go where You want us to go, do what You want us to do and give what You want us to give. We love You LORD, and count it such an honour to be Yours. For King Jesus and for country, we stand on guard.

In Service of the King of Nations (Psalm 72:11)
& a generation yet unborn,

FOREWORD

By Rev. Dr. Alistair Petrie

An individual has a destiny…but what about a nation? Is it possible that a nation carries within its corporate life something that is unique and separate from all the other nations of the world?

Throughout Scripture we find several references to nations that are called, loved, blessed, disciplined, corrected, directed, and even scattered. Well-known passages such as Habakkuk 1:5 indicate that God has purpose and strategy in the way He works with nations – "Look at the nations and watch – and be utterly amazed…". Psalm 33:12 is quite clear in the relationship between a nation and God – "Blessed is the nation whose God is the LORD, the people He chose for His inheritance." In the New Testament, we find further evidence of this unique relationship God has with nations – "From one man He made every nation of men, that they should inhabit the whole earth; and He determined the times set for them and the exact places where they should live" (Acts 17:26-27). Nations – people – have a distinct destiny as determined by God. The Bible itself is a testimony to that very truth – you and I, even cities (c.f. Proverbs 11:10-11), and indeed nations have a future, a hope, a calling, and a destiny.

God has afforded me a profound privilege in allowing me to travel the nations of the world, and to work with their people in helping them to align themselves with the purposes of God. Each time I am away from Canada, however, I look forward to my return. It has been my adopted home for over 45 years. Each time I travel in another nation, I am usually given an open door of welcome for the simple reason that I have come from Canada. There is a uniqueness – an identity – a character…that is clearly Canadian! In more recent years much momentum has developed in identifying what is unique about Canada in relationship to other nations. Simply put, it is a nation that has been called by God for the healing and reconciliation between other nations – as well as the release of destiny of those nations. It can be seen as a spiritual catalyst in the hands of God enabling others to enter their hope and calling.

I am absolutely delighted that Faytene Kryskow has written *Stand On Guard*. This is the first in-depth account I am aware of that clearly accounts for the uniqueness of Canada in its calling and in its purpose as a nation. She has gleaned from history and culture what are the unique components of this land. She has researched what others have written, interpreted political and historical records with care, and has given to us a truly thrilling account of what it means to live in Canada, at a time when there is increasing Divine acceleration throughout the nations, and at a time when others are looking to Canada for clarity and direction.

It is important to read this book carefully – and prayerfully! It is not just a record of historical accounts – but rather living proof that God has designed Canada for a specific purpose. It is not hard to see the Hand of God at work in terms of those who were already here prior to and following Confederation, as well as the principles of life and direction that were spoken into our Constitution. There is a prophetic element to this nation. Our provinces and territories are a composite of the mosaic of God's character and purpose.

In these searching days, we need to know as individuals that we have a hope, a calling and a future. The same principle applies to nations – and I believe Faytene has given us the blueprint that testifies to Canada's spiritual DNA! Take your Bible, some paper and a pen – and prepare to undertake a journey that enables the reader to see through the grid of the Holy Spirit that the destiny of a nation is found in the Hands of the Living God Himself!

Rev. Dr. Alistair P. Petrie
Author
Director - Partnership Ministries,
Kelowna, B.C., Canada

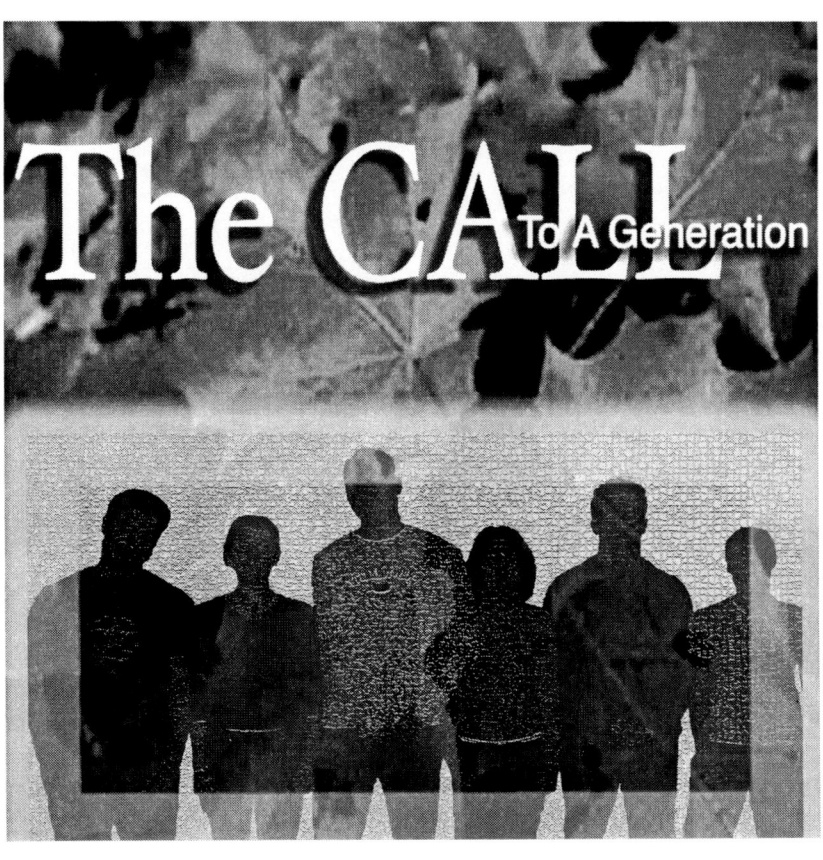

The CALL To A Generation

The LORD looks for a champion...

"So I sought for a man among them who would make a wall, and stand in the gap before Me on behalf of the land." (Ezekiel 22:30a)

...let the Josiah generation arise!

"...Josiah put away those who consulted mediums and spiritists, the household gods and idols, all the abominations that were seen in the land of Judah and in Jerusalem, that he might perform the words of the law which were written in the book that Hilkiah the priest found in the house of the LORD. Now before him there was no king like him, who turned to the LORD with all his heart, with all his soul, and with all his might, according to all the Law of Moses; nor after him did any arise like him."

(2 Kings 23:24-25)

PROPHETIC INTRODUCTION

It has been my honour in the past few years to both witness and be a part of the work of healing that the LORD is doing in the nation of Canada. We are truly living in unprecedented days! As one of the younger persons participating in what the LORD is doing through Watchmen for the Nations[4] in Canada, I want to say that I am **so thankful** to the spiritual fathers and mothers in our day who selflessly give of themselves labouring to see the glory of God rest in our nation. It was at a recent Watchmen for the Nations Gathering that I had a powerful encounter with the Holy Spirit that ultimately led to the book you are now holding. Because of this, I want to begin by sharing that moment, and the revelation that followed, with you as a framework for the entire book.

A GREAT CLOUD OF WITNESSES

In December 2003 I was at a Watchmen for the Nations Gathering in the province of Quebec with leaders from all across Canada. At one point during the Gathering we were in a deep time of corporate prayer where the Holy Spirit had directed us to link arm in arm and kneel as a symbol of our unified heart to see the purposes of God released, in our generation, in Canada. As we knelt, the leader of the meeting, Dr. David Demian, began to speak of the great cloud of witnesses described in Hebrews 12:1. Scripture teaches us that this great cloud of witnesses is composed of saints of old who faithfully served the LORD in their generation even though many did not see the

---

[4]Visit www.watchmen.org for information on what has been happening through Watchmen for the Nations in Canada.

fulfillment of their hopes during their lifetime. Dr. Demian shared with us that he believed there were men and women of God who had laboured for the LORD in Canada in generations past that were looking upon us at that very moment as a part of the great cloud of witnesses:

> *Therefore we also, since we are surrounded by so great a cloud of witnesses, let us lay aside every weight, and sin which so easily ensnares us, and let us run with endurance the race that is set before us, looking unto Jesus, the author and finisher of our faith.* (Hebrews 12:1)

As Dr. Demian spoke I could feel a heavy weight of the LORD's presence. There was such an awesome sense in the room that **we were not alone** but that present with us was an entire heavenly host (I believe both angels and Canadian saints of old) who were looking in on us, from eternity, intently focused on our posture at that moment. We could feel them cheering us on and watching with hope that we would faithfully run our leg of the race. It was both awesome and sobering. In that moment the fear of the LORD filled my heart, as well as a serious awareness of the call to run our leg of the race well, so that, the labours and sacrifice of these saints would not go to waste. The Holy Spirit then began speaking to my heart.

THE RIGHTEOUS FOUNDATIONS OF CANADA: OUR INHERITANCE

He reminded me of how in recent years Christian leaders in the nation had gathered and sought the LORD together, laying down their agendas, and asking for His strategy to see the destiny of Canada realized. As they had sought Him, much of what the Holy Spirit highlighted to them had to do with the historic national sin and disunity issues that needed to be dealt with. The LORD instructed them to begin a journey of healing for Canada that would prepare the nation to be a resting-place for the glory of the LORD, and, propel Canada into His end-time purposes.[5] At this moment, however, and the weeks to follow, I felt the LORD highlighting another strategic directive for the Body of Christ in Canada. What He said to my heart was this:

> *Along with Canada's unrighteous history, which does require healing, there is also a RIGHTEOUS history to reclaim. There are righteous foundations that have been laid up by your forefathers. They are an inheritance for you. I am looking for a generation that will rise up and begin to lay hold of this righteous inheritance. I am looking for a generation that will reclaim the righteous foundations of Canada.*

"There is also a righteous inheritance to reclaim."

I then had a vision. In the vision I saw the righteous foundations He had just spoken to my heart regarding. They were covered over with dust and dirt and buried out of plain sight. All of a sudden a dusting broom from Heaven appeared and began to clean them off so that they became clearly visible. Through this vision the LORD was speaking to my heart that He was looking to reveal, or bring into clear view, righteous foundations in the nation that had become hidden over time. I sensed that He was asking me to be one of those who would, by Heaven's grace and guidance, work to "dust" these foundations off, and bring them to the attention of the current generation[6] so that we could work to reclaim and steward them. It was like He was saying:

> *I am looking for a generation to reclaim and stand on these righteous foundations but there is a problem. The problem is this: many do not even know that these foundations are there! How can they reclaim what they do not see or even*

---

[5] See the prophecy from Yonggi Cho on page 116 for an encouraging word along the same theme. Also, again, see www.watchmen.org.

[6] The use of the terms **current generation** is meant to include all those who are alive in Canada at this time in history, it does not refer to a specific age group.

know exists? How can they be faithful to steward what they
do not even comprehend is their possession?

Then, to help me understand, the Holy Spirit gave this analogy. He said,

Many in your generation in Canada are like the grandchildren of extremely wealthy stock. They have a massive inheritance only they have no idea that their grandparents set it aside for them and that it is even buried in their own backyard! There is a vault full of funds that has been stored for them but, for the most part, they have no suspicion that it is even there! Because of this the funds are just sitting, buried, and wasting.[7] The inheritance was put there by their ancestors for them to use and build with in this generation.

The Holy Spirit was clearly speaking to my heart that now is the time for the grandchildren to realize what rightfully belongs to them, get the vault location, lock combination, a shovel, and begin digging to find the inheritance! Once the inheritance is found they will be able to use it to build in their generation and then re-invest for the generation to come.

On the heels of this analogy the LORD began speaking to my heart regarding His nature as a covenant keeping God.

---

[7] I believe this is especially the case with my age range (thirty) and under. Those in this age group have grown up with VERY little sense of our righteous history in this nation.

THE BIBLICAL MODEL OF COVENANT INHERITANCE: ABRAHAM, ISAAC AND JACOB

The LORD is a covenant keeper. All throughout scripture He is referred to as the God of Abraham, Isaac, and Jacob. I believe one of the reasons for this was to remind the Israelites that the covenant established between God and Abraham was given as an inheritance to Abraham's sons, Isaac and Jacob also. It belonged to them because it had been established between the LORD and their father, Abraham. Furthermore, the LORD's covenant with Abraham (Genesis 12 and 22) was officially renewed with Isaac (Genesis 26) and then with Jacob (Genesis 28). For the covenant renewal, the LORD initiated, and Jacob and Isaac willingly responded. In a similar way, I sensed the LORD saying that He was giving an invitation to our generation in Canada to renew covenant with Him and walk in a relational commitment, with Him, as our righteous forefathers had.

Then the LORD spoke four words to my heart: "Agreement of the Ages."

Why did God bless Isaac abundantly? Why did He show Jacob such favour? It was because of the covenant He had with Abraham! This is how God works. He is into generational inheritance — He is a covenant keeping King!

The LORD then spoke four words to my heart:

"AGREEMENT OF THE AGES."

AGREEMENT OF THE AGES

After I heard these words I had another vision. In this second vision, I saw righteous Canadians from the founding generation of the nation and then all the successive generations lined one beside the other in historical order. At the end of the line was the current generation — **us.** All of a sudden our generation began to rise up and reach through time for the righteous foundations that had been laid up by all the previous generations. When we found them we firmly gripped them and began to pull them forth, literally, through time. The way we did this was by **agreeing with them in heart, principle, action and prayer**. As we came into agreement with these righteous foundations they were reestablished with great power in our generation because of their historical weight. It was amazing and awesome! Before my eyes, in the Spirit, an "Agreement of the Ages" that had tremendous authority had just been demonstrated! It was incredible!

As we came into agreement with these righteous foundations they were reestablished with great power in our generation because of their historical weight.

The LORD then reminded me of how we function in an "Agreement of the Ages" every time we pray "He will have dominion from sea to sea" (Psalm 72:8, the verse that inspired the Founding Fathers to name Canada the "Dominion of Canada"). It is easy to sense an added authority when we quote this scripture while praying for Canada. I believe this authority is because of Psalm 72's direct link to our nation's foundation. The LORD honours what He established by His Spirit through generations past. As such, the LORD honours what He established by His Spirit through the Fathers of Confederation in Canada. In these moments of revelation I sensed that there were *more* spiritual foundations like this one (Psalm 72) that had been laid. At this time I also had an inkling that significant indications of what was in the heart of Canada at its foundation would be found in the newspapers of 1867.[8]

---

[8] See Chapter 3.

34

INCREASED ANOINTING THROUGH GENERATIONAL AGREEMENT

Over the months, as I meditated further on what God had been speaking to my heart about the "Agreement of the Ages," I realized that this was a clear biblical principle.

Matthew 18:19 explains:

Again I say to you that if two of you agree on earth concerning anything that they ask, it will be done for them by My Father in heaven.

There is great power in agreement.

Furthermore, in recent days I had noticed an incredible increase in anointing at prayer meetings where members of different age groups came into agreement with one another for righteousness sake. At one particular meeting, the LORD led a cluster of "Gen-Xers" to come into agreement with some "Baby-Boomers" for a move of the Spirit reminiscent of the Latter Rain Revival (1948). The anointing was very heavy and the authority was very powerful — surprisingly powerful! In the weeks that followed we saw the direct fruit of this prayer at some meetings where the Holy Spirit visited large groups of young people in an extraordinary way. Through this experience the Holy Spirit was teaching me that there is great authority released when the generations come into agreement with one another for righteousness sake. "There the LORD commands a blessing – Life forevermore!" (Psalm 133:3).

There is great authority released when generations come into agreement with one another for righteousness sake.

What He was speaking to my heart about Canada was simply an extension of the biblical principle of the power of agreement. As our generation agreed with that which was set in place by generations past it would be loosed on earth with great authority and effect. Because of this principle of agreement, finding the **dusted over foundations**

would mean a release of great spiritual ammunition for our generation. He was speaking to my heart that these foundations were hidden weapons of mass destruction against the works of darkness in Canada! Again, I felt the deep longing of the LORD for a new generation (composed of young and old alike) to arise in unity and reestablish these foundations.

Again, I felt the deep longing of the LORD for a new generation to arise in unity and reestablish these foundations.

Almost immediately I set my face like flint to find, and dust off, some of these foundations. Along the way came significant confirmations of this revelation, and an exhortation that, I believe, is important to share as a preamble to the actual research.

PROPHETIC CONFIRMATIONS

My challenge was this: God was downloading all of this revelation but my day-timer was stacked with ministry related engagements that left little or no time for writing. Along with this, I am not a trained writer. Putting this publication together would be a real challenge. At the same time I did not want to "miss God" as it felt like this was a "**now**" word for Canada. Because of this, I looked for a confirmation. Within weeks

I did not want to "miss God" as it felt like this was a "now" word

encouragement came from two strong prophetic individuals in the nation who said, "*Write the book.*" That is pretty clear! Days after this, my friend Noah Scott[9] shared with me a powerful dream he had recently had. As he described his dream the Holy Spirit came upon me and I began to weep because of the presence of God on what he shared. It was an amazing confirmation.

---

[9] Noah Scott is the Associate Director of the Vancouver Healing Rooms.

NOAH'S DREAM

In the dream Noah was in an old house. It was in good shape but was totally abandoned. He began walking up a set of stairs in the house where all along the walls there were drawers. As he walked up the stairs he opened each drawer with the hopes of finding something of value. Drawer after drawer he opened and looked inside but found nothing. At the top of the stairs he entered a loft and, after surveying it, his eyes came to an old dresser with a framed photo

I will take the baton and fight for righteousness and justice in this generation

on top. This photo depicted an army general from days past and Noah could tell from the many medals and ribbons on his coat that this was a general of great honour.

As Noah looked at the picture he began to weep and this revelation filled his thoughts:

You fought and gave your whole life to fight in your generation for what is right and just. You paid such a great price but no one — NO ONE — not even your own family has picked up the baton that you had to pass on. Even though none of them were willing to pick up your baton, I will do it. I will do it! I will fight. I will take the baton and fight for righteousness and justice in this generation. I will fight.

Next he felt compelled to open the top drawer of the dresser. This time he found something inside — a ring box. With excitement Noah opened it and saw that mounted inside the box was a huge signet ring. His heart sunk with the realization that the ring was at least 3 to 4 times the size of his finger and that, though he had a desire to put it on, it would never fit him. Nevertheless, something told him to try. He slipped it onto his finger and, to his amazement, he saw that it fit perfectly!

What the LORD was saying to our generation through this dream seemed clear. There is a call. **There is a position of battle for** righteousness and justice that He is looking for a generation to take up in the spirit as generations past did. There is an authority that we are being given to fight with in this generation (signified by the General of honour (an accomplished fighter from days past) and then the signet ring (authority)). If we choose to take it the LORD will give us the ability to carry His authority even though it appears to be too big for us (signified by the ring that looked too big but, in actuality, fit perfectly). **He will give us grace and authority to do what He has called us to — grace and authority to fight for, and reestablish righteousness in the nation. He is only looking for a generation of mighty men and women who will, once again, take up the call and lay down their lives.**

He is only looking for a generation of mighty men and women who will, once again, take up the call and lay down their lives.

ENCOUNTER ON THE PLAINS OF ABRAHAM

Seven months after I began "dusting" in research I was at another national Gathering of Christian leaders in Quebec: the Homecoming.[10] The purpose of the Homecoming was to bring healing to the root issues of brokeness between France and French speaking Canada. During this Gathering all of the leaders present assembled on the Plains of Abraham for a time of prayer and reconciliation. On this field, where the fate of our nation was determined in 1759, a representative of Christian leaders in the nation stood and made a covenant before the LORD. We swore as Louis de Buade de

---

[10] See www.watchmen.org for more information about this Gathering and the related history between France and French speaking Canada.

Frontenac, one of our spiritual forefathers, did, saying:

As for me I shall esteem myself happy in consecrating all my efforts and, if need be, my life itself to extending the empire of Jesus Christ throughout this land.[11]

Like my experience at the December 2003 Gathering, this moment was extremely powerful and sobering. As we stood there and made a commitment to enter into the same level of sacrifice for Canada that Frontenac had, I was acutely aware that I was unable, with my natural mind, to fully comprehend the magnitude of what was happening in the spirit realm at that moment. The power released at our corporate commitment was massive! It was all too HUGE for my mental understanding. Later, when someone at the Homecoming asked me what I was feeling about everything the LORD was doing in our midst, all I could think to say was:

The power released at our corporate commitment was massive!

I feel like a ladybug on the space shuttle! I know I have boarded a very powerful transport vehicle in the spirit realm. I am aware that we are riding on something very huge but I do not fully comprehend it with my natural mind. All I know is that my spirit man is very in tune with the magnitude of all this for Canada. I know the LORD is here "driving" this thing, I know that this is extremely significant and I just feel so honoured, and humbled, to be here.

As the crowd of leaders began to disperse from the field I had a strong "God-brooding" sense that the LORD had something more to say to me. So I put down my belongings and did what felt appropriate: I lay prostrate, face down, on the grass. Without realizing it at that moment, I believe this was a strong prophetic statement. As I lay there on the Plains, with my face in the sod (where many soldiers had spilled their blood centuries ago), these words began to flood my mind:

*Many men, many men, **MANY MEN** right here on this field willingly sacrificed their lives for the sake of a land they*

---

[11] See page 95 regarding Louis de Buade de Frontenac.

called home. They considered their lives as nothing to be grasped — nothing — and willingly gave their lives for the land to which they were committed. Again, I [the LORD] am looking for a generation that will count their lives as nothing to see what they believe in established and preserved in this nation — to see righteousness established in this generation in Canada.

It was like He was speaking to my heart, *"Your draft number is up. What is your decision?"* Suddenly, a prayer began to come out of a very deep place in my spirit, *"My life is not my own. I belong to Your purposes LORD and I will give my life, with full recognition of the high cost, for the sake of Your name and this nation."* At that time something extremely powerful was imparted into my spirit. From that moment on it seemed like the flag of Canada was running (almost literally) through my blood. I felt tied to this nation at a depth that was so intense it was overwhelming at times. In the midst of the intensity, **I was consoled with the knowledge that what I was experiencing was not just about me – it was about a generation.** It was like God was saying He was at work in me (and many others across the land I'm sure) as a picture of **what He wanted to do with our entire generation in Canada.**[12]

"Your draft number is up. What is your decision?"

Two weeks later I was in the airport at the nation's capital, Ottawa, on my way to speak at an Inuit youth conference in Nunavik (the north of Quebec). While waiting for my ride, the spirit of prophecy came upon me with great intensity. Following is a word that I received in that moment. At the time I did not see the direct connection to the Plains of Abraham experience, I thought it was a word solely for the Inuit youth, however, I see the clear link now.

---

[12] Some in the Body of Christ call this type of experience prophetic burden bearing or prophetic intercession. Whatever you call it, it is very powerful.

A VISION OF BOND SERVANTS

I saw a vision of an earlobe being pierced and I knew immediately the LORD was bringing my attention to the Hebrew practice of ear-piercing slaves who had declared lifetime devotion to one master. In Exodus 21 the LORD instructed the Hebrews regarding this practice. He said:

If you buy a Hebrew servant, he shall serve you six years; and in the seventh he shall go out free and pay nothing. If he comes in by himself, he shall go out by himself; if he comes in married, then his wife shall go out with him. If his master has given him a wife, and she has borne him sons or daughters, the wife and her children shall be her master's and he shall go out by himself. But if the servant plainly says, 'I love my master, my wife, and my children; I will not go out free,' then his master shall bring him to the judges. He shall also bring him to the door, or to the doorpost, and his master shall pierce his ear with an awl and he shall serve him forever (Exodus 21: 1-6).

Then the LORD expanded:

I AM LOOKING FOR A PEOPLE

I have shown you this at this time because I am releasing a call to consecration upon my Body — a call to be completely devoted to Me, the LORD God Almighty, King of the entire universe. There is a "mark" and there is a piercing that is the mark of those who will not only receive from the benefits of My Cross (that is salvation) but of those that will bear the marks of sacrifice and enter into the fellowship of the sufferings of the Cross. For this is, and will be, the mark of true spiritual authority in the land. It is not something to be taken lightly, says the LORD, but to be regarded with the utmost humility and reverence. For I, the LORD, am Holy and pure

41

and, though I am the King of salvation, it was salvation bought through great sacrifice — the sacrifice of the Cross. So again, I am calling to my Chosen Ones: Be Holy as I am Holy. Walk as I would walk. Walk holy, and wholly, unto the LORD. The marks of the faithful saints are the marks of sacrifice. I remind you, it is through My wounds that healing poured, and continues to pour, forth.

I AM LOOKING FOR THOSE WHO WILL LAY DOWN THEIR LIVES

*So again, I call to a generation that will lay down their lives and consider all things as **nothing** compared to knowing Me. The road is narrow and the gate is low. I am looking for those who will humble themselves and enter into My sufferings for the sake of this land once again. For in the days of old, My men and women of might came to this nation and they laid down their lives — LITERALLY — to see My dominion established in this land. The forces of darkness contended against them but they did not consider their lives as anything to be grasped. In humility, they laid down their lives for this nation. They laid down their lives for a land that they did not even know would one day be called Canada. They laboured and toiled, they counted the cost, they took the wounds and they bore the scars to do My bidding in this nation. And now, again, I look to and fro across the lengths of this land searching for those whose hearts are wholly committed to Me, as these ones' were, that I might again send my people into new lands and new realms of destiny and glory.*

WHO WILL PIONEER FOR
RIGHTEOUSNESS SAKE?

For I desire to raise up a host that will carry a pioneering missionary spirit for this land once again. *Those who will carry My word and mandate to the lost in all the regions of culture, says the LORD.* *I desire to send my chosen and faithful ones into the arts, entertainment, news, educational systems, media and medical realms, says the LORD.* *I am searching for those upon whom I might lay My mantle for this nation;* *those who will not love their lives unto death but will go for the glory of My name.* *Where is the place where I might dwell?* *Who is the one that will willingly go and be a light in the darkness?* *Who will go and stand as a tower of righteousness for Me in the midst of this generation?* *Where is the house you will build for Me?* *Long have I desired to dwell and take "Dominion" — but who will go — whom shall I send?* *Who will go for Me?*

PRAYER MOVEMENT
WITH BODY MOVEMENT

The LORD downloaded these words like a waterfall into my soul. I then began to think about how, in recent years, we have seen an incredible prayer mobilization across Canada. As a nation we are deeply indebted to ministries like Canada in Prayer, Prayer Canada, the House of Prayer movement, the Canadian Prayer Network, Operation Prayer Watch and others who have given tremendous leadership to streams and moves of intercession across Canada. We are also indebted to ministries like 100 Huntley Street, Women's Aglow, End-time Handmaidens, Campus Crusade for Christ, Watchmen for the Nations (the Canadian Prayer Shield) who, though their mandates extend beyond prayer, have also mobilized multitudes

43

to intercession for Canada. All these, and others, have been paving a highway in the spirit to prepare the way for the LORD. Intense battles have been fought in prayer, ground has been taken, and ground has been held. It has been my privilege to labour in some of these streams and, as already mentioned, I am so thankful for those who have given leadership to them. Many have paid a high cost. But let me tell you something: I hear a trumpet call that has an added tune in this hour! The LORD is calling His Church not only to pray that He will have dominion but also to **boldly GO** and establish His dominion in every arena of the nation!

This is in no way to say that the call to national prayer mobilization is over, or even diminishing. That would be a ludicrous statement to make! Intercession will never be over as long as there is one realm on the planet that is under the dominion of Satan. Even then, we must pray to maintain the ground we have taken! If anything, I believe we must increase in desperate, fervent, and strategic prayer for Canada. I simply believe God is saying prayer alone is not enough — we must GO and possess the nation for the LORD. There has to be a point at which we begin to be the answer to our prayers in this nation. There needs to be a point where we begin to rise up in faith and execute, by the LORD's grace, favour, and guidance, the very things for which we are travailing.

There needs to be a point where we begin to rise up in faith and execute, by the LORD'S grace, favour and guidance, the very things for which we are travailing.

Since this prophetic download in the Ottawa airport, I have been consumed with a word to this generation in Canada — a strong call to *possess the gates of influence* in our nation for righteousness sake. I believe this word gives part of the LORD's strategy to see the righteous foundations of Canada reestablished in our day. Let me explain.

Possess the gates of influence in our nation for righteousness sake.

THE TERM "GATES"

In the Old Testament "gates" were places of great influence. At the gates of a city #1) those who held positions of authority gathered to make decisions and #2) what went "in" and "out" of the city was regulated. Whoever possessed the gates of a walled city controlled that city. This is why the covenant promise given to Abraham by the LORD in Genesis 22:17, that his descendants would "possess the gate of their enemies," was so incredible! In essence what the LORD was saying to Him was: *"Abraham, I am going to give your children total authority over their enemies and over the regions that their enemies have controlled in the past. These enemies will have NO influence or authority over your children, or your children's children!"* What an awesome promise!

In the context of the exhortation I am about to share with you, the use of the term "gates" simply means those places of greatest influence in our nation. **"Gates" include any and every avenue by which a generation's mindsets, codes, cultural values, moral standards, and the like are determined or influenced. They are the places of greatest impartation into the soul of a nation and generation.**

POSSESSING THE GATES OF INFLUENCE

It is my perception that often in recent history, when a person has had zeal to lay down their lives in order to see the Kingdom of God established in their generation, that they would dedicate themselves to full time "Christian" service. I feel strongly however that, in the current generation, the wind of the Holy Spirit is blowing many of His "marked ones" who carry His genuine authority in a different, and **strategic**, direction. This is nothing new for Canada. It is something that our forefathers understood and walked in with great commitment.

Let me give you just a few, of many possible, examples:[13]

- **Explorers and Cartographers**: Jaques Cartier, Samuel de Champlain, and David Thompson excelled in their day as explorers and cartographers of the New World. The motivation for their exploration was to glorify God and advance the gospel.

- **Entrepreneurs:** Sieur de Monts was a successful businessman and entrepreneur (today we might call him a marketplace apostle). He, and other successful business people from France, committed their lives and finances to advancing the gospel in New France (early Canada).

- **Teachers, Nurses and Nuns:** Marie Guyart de l'Incarnation was teacher, nurse and nun who, at great personal sacrifice, laboured faithfully in obedience to a dream in which the LORD told her to go to Canada to build a house for Jesus and preach the gospel to the First Nations! **Marie helped provide the best education and health care of the time in New France.** She worked with several other committed nuns who laboured in the same way with great love for God, the First Nations and for the new settlement.

- **Politician(s) and Journalist:** George Brown was one of the Founding Fathers of Confederation and was also founder of the Toronto Globe & Mail. Brown, Samuel Tilley, Oliver Mowat and others like them, worked to influence the nation for righteousness sake in politics during the nation's founding years. Along with this, Brown utilized his platform in media for the LORD. He gave great glory to God in his editorial writing regarding the affairs of the nation.

---

[13] Chapters 1 and 2 are dedicated completely to presenting inspiring examples of the lives of Canadians who took a stand for Christ in their various "gates" of influence. This introduction lists only a sampling of the many possible examples.

- **Educators:** Bishop John Strachan and Egerton Ryerson were pioneers in the Canadian educational system. They both endeavored to set a standard in Canadian education that would place the cross at the centre of all learning.

There were many others who stood faithfully in their "gates" for righteousness sake. Individuals such as:

- Marguerite Bourgeouys, New France's first **schoolmistress.**

- Paul de Chomedey de Maisonneuve**, co-founder of the city of Montréal.**

- Jeanne Mance, **founder of Montréal's first hospital.**

- Louis Riel, **justice advocate** and **Father of Manitoba.**

- Henry Bird Steinhauer, Ojibway **missionary** and **translator.**

- William Howland, **businessman** and **Mayor** of Toronto.

- Nellie McClung, best selling **author.**

- Timothy Eaton, successful **entrepreneur.**

- Agnes MacPhail, first female **Member of Parliament.**

- George P. Vanier, **Governor General.**

This list could go on for pages. All these individuals tenaciously rose up in their respective spheres of influence for the glory of God.

The LORD is looking to raise up righteous nation shakers and people of influence in our generation as in days past. I believe most of them will have their impact outside of the walls of traditional church structures. Of course, there will always be those the LORD raises up into full-time Christian service to equip and encourage the Body of Christ. But beyond this, I believe the LORD is wanting to raise up a host of apostles, prophets, evangelists, teachers and pastors (yes — five fold offices!) that will possess every gate of influence in our nation. **These mighty men and women of God will regulate what goes "in" and "out" of our land with righteous, God fearing, discernment. They will be ones who will "stand" with true spiritual authority and turn the tide in Canada through their influence in the arts, communications, politics, science, sports, industry, the marketplace, education, medicine, law and in EVERY ARENA OF INFLUENCE IN OUR NATION.**

They will be ones who will "stand" with true spiritual authority and turn the tide in Canada.

For the last few decades it would appear that the enemy has had one up on the Church in this particular tactic of spiritual warfare (i.e. possessing the gates of influence). He has craftily groomed and raised up ones that would speak for him in every arena of influence in our nation. In recent decades they seem to be doing their "gatekeeping" job with finesse (for clarity sake: I am not saying that ones who have been used unrighteously to influence the nation are the enemy — Satan alone is our only enemy. Those he uses are victims themselves and we need to pray that they will be released from his grip and used more mightily for God than they were for the kingdom of darkness).

Now is the time! **Now is the time to possess the gates of influence in our land for righteousness sake just as many of our forefathers did!** Now is the time to consider our lives as nothing and to begin to aggressively take back what the enemy has tried to convince us is his domain when it is not!

Now is the time to possess the gates of influence in the land for righteousness sake just as many of our forefathers did!

THE NATIONAL INTIMIDATION

I believe Satan has taken great care in attempts to weaken and intimidate this generation of the Church in Canada. I believe he has tried to make us mentally submit to and verbally agree with the statement: Canada is a Godless nation. He has tried to make the Church of Jesus Christ in this nation believe, or at least feel, that we are the "underdogs" and that the expression of our faith is to be left to Sunday morning services. On the basis of the historical and foundational facts of Canada, the belief that the Church has no place in national affairs is faulty!

First of all, the earliest European settlers who planted their roots in the land that would one day be called "The Dominion of Canada" were missionaries from France. The LORD commissioned these ones under the auspices of the King of France **to establish a Christian colony that would bring the gospel of Jesus Christ to the First Nations.** Many of these

They came to establish a Christian colony.

missionaries had clear dreams and visions from the Spirit of God divinely commissioning them to come to the "New Land."[14] These initial settlers paid a high price to plant their roots here. **Some even gave their lives in martyrdom** because of the vision that burned in their hearts.[15] In these early years a bounty of gospel seeds were planted and, especially after the first Christian martyrdom, many First Nations readily accepted Jesus Christ.

The Fathers of Confederation clearly gave Jesus Christ access to the affairs of the nation.

A few centuries later, several leaders forged the way to Confederation. Many of these men were God-fearing. They tenaciously laboured to see the name of the LORD set into the foundations of the new union. During this process, **the Fathers of Confederation clearly gave**

---

[14] See page 84 regarding Marie Guyart de l'Incarnation.
[15] See pages 80-84 regarding Jean de Brebeuf and the Jesuits.

Jesus Christ access to the affairs of the nation when they chose to declare that "He will have dominion also from sea to sea..." (Psalm 72:8). **They set this decree into our very NAME when they chose to call Canada the "DOMINION of Canada."** Job 22:28, speaking to those who fear the LORD, says, "You will declare [decree] a thing, and it will be established for you." These men of God overtly established our destiny and standard as a nation: **HE WILL HAVE DOMINION.**

I believe our first Prime Minister, Sir John A. Macdonald, articulated this best in his letter to the Queen of England explaining why the Fathers of Confederation wanted to call the new nation, "The Dominion of Canada." Macdonald explained to the Queen that the word "dominion" was taken directly from Psalm 72:8 and that, *"the name was a tribute to the principles they earnestly desired to uphold."*[16] Let history speak: The LORD was given clear invitation into this nation's affairs at our birth!

Our forefathers set a precedent for the Church to stand in and walk out with confidence in our day. When we hear the enemy whisper, "Face it, Canada is a Godless nation. Christians have no right to influence the affairs of Canada. Christianity belongs inside the walls of a church building on Sunday mornings and nowhere else," we need to recognize it for what it is: *INTIMIDATION!*

> *When we hear the enemy whisper...we need to recognize it for what it is: INTIMIDATION.*

If the enemy has tried to intimidate the Canadian Church into an underdog mentality in our nation, we need to wake up and realize a few things. First of all, we are the head and not the tail in Christ, we are above and not beneath because of the covenantal blessing of God on our lives (Deuteronomy 28:13). As the Church we are seated in

---

[16] See page 121 regarding Sir Leonard Tilley.

50

heavenly places above every power and principality that seeks to exalt itself above the LORD (Ephesians 1:12, 3:10, 6:12). We are more than conquerors in Christ (Romans 3:37). There is no such thing as underdog status when we are in Christ! It does not exist! Secondly, Jesus Christ has legitimately been invited to come into and have dominion over all our affairs as a

It is our responsibility to remind the nation of our inheritance, violently call it forth in the spirit, STAND in it and possess it!

nation. As the Church in this generation it is our responsibility to remind the nation of our inheritance, violently call it forth in the spirit, STAND in it, and possess it!

Furthermore, Satan is not the creator. That means the arts, technology and science do not belong to him. He is not the healer. This means medicine does not belong to him, nor should its system. He is not a just ruler, therefore the justice system is not his to possess. He is not the author of wisdom and intelligence, therefore he should not have access to our education systems. The only reason he can possess these gates of influence in our nation is if we, the Church, abdicate our role as stewards of righteousness in them.

We need to boldly arise and receive the mantle the LORD is seeking to lay upon this generation. A mantle to walk in the example left by the founding missionaries and Founding Fathers of the land as they walked in the example of Christ. They left such a rich inheritance in the spirit. The LORD has stationed us, His Church in this generation, as stewards of His righteousness. **Not only do we have legal access through the spiritual inheritance laid up by our**

forefathers but we have a clear Kingdom mandate from the LORD! It's time to reclaim and stand for righteousness in our day!

So this is the challenge:

1) Let's get zealous for the glory of the LORD's name in Canada!
2) Let's get mobilized!

THE CALL

To the emerging Christian generation in Canada I feel the LORD is saying: **"Believe big!"** No realm of influence is too large for the LORD! He is LORD over all! We must remember Joseph, Esther, and Daniel, who were raised up with great favour and influence in their generation by the LORD's hand. He used them to establish righteous systems and decrees in the land. We must remember King Josiah (I believe we are a Josiah generation) who, when he found the law that was given to his forefathers through the prophet Moses, fell on his face before the LORD, rallied the people, tore down the places of idol worship and called the nation to honour, worship, and revere the LORD. It was an "Agreement of the Ages" maneuver that King Josiah executed! Josiah looked to the righteousness covenant that generations past had with the LORD and reestablished it for the nation in his day (see 2 Kings 22 and 23).

"Believe big!" No realm of influence is too large for the LORD! He is LORD over all!

Go! Shake the medical system for Jesus! Shake the political system for Jesus! Shake the music world for Jesus! Shake the national (and international!) economic scene for Jesus! Shake the legal system for Jesus! Shake all the gates of influence in this nation and generation for Jesus!! If we don't, who will? God's arm is not too short! With God we are more than able. Can you see it? Can you feel it? (I know I am preaching now — I feel like I am going to explode with the truth of this word!) We **cannot** be intimidated in this hour. The stakes are too high! We are fighting for the soul of our nation and for future generations. There **truly is** a great cloud of witnesses looking on

Shake all the gates of influence in this nation for Jesus!! If we don't, who will?

from heaven. They are cheering us on in our leg of the race. They laid down their lives for the LORD and for us. Now it is our turn.

WORD OF WISDOM:
STEWARDSHIP & REVOLUTION

In all this, I have also felt the LORD speaking to my heart a word of wisdom. This word wisdom is regarding STEWARDSHIP and REVOLUTION. The LORD spoke to my heart that in the areas in which the previous generations walked in righteousness before the LORD and upheld the righteous foundations of the land we are to honour them and faithfully steward what they established. Exodus 20:12 clearly teaches that when we honour our fathers and mothers we will be blessed and will live long in the land the Lord has given us as an inheritance. We must honour, bless and give thanks for the work they that they have done and the ground they have taken.

We must honour, bless and give thanks for the work that they have done and the ground they have taken.

This is exactly what King Josiah did. He honoured what was established between the LORD and his forefather Moses and then he laboured, wholeheartedly, to uphold Israel's covenant before the LORD in his generation. He stewarded his inheritance and stood in his gate faithfully. In doing so he preserved both a generation and a nation in righteousness. This principle of stewardship was also demonstrated by King Solomon who took the inheritance left by His father, David and used it to build a temple for the LORD in His generation. King David paid the price for the temple materials but it was King Solomon who stewarded these materials and actually brought to birth the fullness of his father's dream.

There are many areas in the nation where righteousness has been sown and stored up. Now it is our time to build with the Godly materials they prepared and take it to the next level for the glory of

Now it is our time to build with the Godly materials they prepared and take it to the next level for the glory of God!

God! Conversely, where previous generations failed to uphold the righteous foundations of the nation there is a radical call for us to arise in a REVOLUTIONARY SPIRIT to overthrow the areas of unrighteousness in the land and see the name of the LORD honoured in every gate of influence. King Josiah understood this as well. He violently overthrew ALL the wickedness that had gained territory in Israel. The LORD is calling us to do the same in Canada! I know this is all sounding political — it is! That realm belongs to Jesus too!

There is a radical call for us to arise in a REVOLUTIONARY SPIRIT to overthrow the areas of unrighteousness in the land.

GET ZEALOUS: REVOLUTIONARIES ARISE!

I have to confess that my prayer focus for the leadership of the nation has shifted dramatically in the last 6 months. The change came as I heard a strong prophetic word spoken through recognized prophetess, Cindy Jacobs.[17] In this word (released in early 2004), she prophesied that it would be the next generation in Canada that would begin to rise up in a revolutionary spirit to demand righteousness from the government. Prior to this my strategy in praying for the leadership of the nation was most often to pray for the current leadership of the land. I prayed that they would make righteous decisions, that they would walk in the fear of the LORD, that they would know Jesus, that they work to see the dominion of Jesus Christ established from sea to sea as our forefathers purposed. When I heard

---

[17] For more information on Cindy Jacobs' ministry see www.generals.org.

this word through Cindy Jacobs however, something powerful erupted in my spirit. I realized that strategic intercession must include

Call forth the "Dread Champions" of the LORD.

praying to call forth the "Dread Champions"[18] of the LORD that He is raising up in the *emerging* leadership of the nation. It is time to call forth the ones who will have **no fear** but will boldly rise up and demand righteousness in all realms of society! We must call forth those who will be radical in this generation and will radically possess the gates of influence for righteousness sake! Those who will rise in a spirit like that which was on Jehu! Jehu was not intimidated by King Ahab, or his sorceress wife Jezebel, but responded with righteous zeal to the call of God on His life, confronted Jezebel and thereby cleansed the land of her idolatrous influence (2 Kings 9:30-37).

GET MOBILIZED:
INTERCESSORS & RESOURCERS

For too long the enemy has had a monopoly on the gates of influence in Canada. We must not tolerate his influence in the gates of the nation any longer. You may not be called

We must become strategic resourcers.

to stand as a leader in one of the realms of influence in society (though perhaps you are and just do not know it yet) but, whoever you are, you definitely have a significant role to play. As those who intercede for Canada we need to begin to pray, not only for ones in current national leadership, but also for the *emerging* generation of leaders. We must soak them in our intercession, praying that their paths will be bathed with favour, wisdom, and grace. Secondly, we must become strategic resourcers. I beseech

---

[18] This use of this term here refers to prophetic exhortations in recent years regarding a radical army of righteous warriors that the LORD would be raising up at this time in history. To review this word visit the prophetic archives at www.extremeprophetic.com.

you, begin to look in your youth groups, in your college groups, in your university groups and in unsuspecting places – in your seniors groups (this is not an age thing)!

Ask the LORD to show you who He has marked and is raising up to be a strong pioneer for righteousness sake in Canada. Perhaps the LORD will show you a young woman called to influence the media or music industry for righteousness sake. Perhaps He will show you a middle aged man called to influence the law system for righteousness sake, perhaps an older person who has a destiny yet to be fulfilled in the political arena of the nation — let us look for them. You may be very surprised at who He leads you to. Once we find them let us rise up and sow into them! Let us sow into them with encouragement, prayer, finances, and by opening doors for them wherever and whenever the LORD leads. Let us set one another up to successfully possess the gates of influence all across this nation! We must realize that we are in this TOGETHER. When one succeeds we all succeed because we are one Body — His Body. It is time to invest strategically into the call of God on one another's lives — for the sake of our King and His Kingdom.

Let us set one another up to successfully possess the gates of influence all across this nation!

A GREAT EXAMPLE

I was so blessed recently to hear of an elderly man, with financial resources, who is doing just this. He is strategically seeking out strong Christian high school students of proven character who have a desire to teach in the Canadian school system. This incredible man gives multiple thousands every year to pay the university tuition of righteous radicals that are going to stand for truth in the gates of influence!

Along the same vein, I just met a group of young radicals for Jesus with real musical skill and anointing. By the leading of the

LORD they have all quit their jobs and are living by faith in order to pursue making an influence for Jesus in the music world. They testified to me how a few people around them discerned the genuine call on their lives and began sowing prayerfully and financially into them. That is awesome!

I praise God for spiritual fathers and mothers of vision like these and pray for many more to catch this vision and strategy. I believe this makes a break from our recent corporate history as a nation. All too often, when righteous radicals have begun to rise in various gates of influence in the nation, they have been criticized, misunderstood, slandered and intimidated to death by those who should have protected, shielded, given grace and supported them in the call. Again, we need to realize that when one wins we all win — and most importantly, the Kingdom is advanced! Who cares whom God has chosen to use? Let us be thankful that He has found someone who has responded with the courage and boldness to go for it! We have such an awesome opportunity to pray for and invest in those who are still in potential form.

How will a seed of potential grow if it is not watered and put into good soil? Unless the right ingredients are provided it will only remain a seed of potential. The fruit of that seed will not grow unless it is one of a few exceptional "die-hard" seeds of which, by the grace of God, I believe there *We must stand,* are always some. But let us not leave the die-*together, as one* hards stranded in their pioneering pursuit of *body in this day.* righteousness! Let us strategically raise up an army — a generation! We must **stand**, **together**, as the Body of Christ in this day. The call is too large for one man or woman. The LORD has designed us to be a Body in which every joint supplies. It is our destiny to work together so let us arise, together, and build!

It is our hour to reclaim through the prayer of agreement and through aggressive action what the enemy has attempted to steal. It is our hour to stand for the King of Glory in this nation, Jesus

Christ, and for a generation yet unborn! The only way we lose the battle is if we neglect to show up with a fight in our heart.

I believe the call is clear and the time is now.
I believe I felt a strong call to write this book at this time for a reason — I believe this is a now word.

For the sake of a nation
For the name of the LORD
For the sake of a generation
Yet unborn
> *I will fight*
>> *I will stand*
Will there be brother beside me?
Sister in view?
Whatever the measure
If many or few
> *Still—I will fight*
>> *Still—I will stand*
There's a roar in my spirit
A fire in my bones
With eyes lifted to heaven
I find my console
> *And I fight*
>> *And I stand*
So, I pray on that glorious morn
When my face meets yours LORD
On my sleeve will read "faithful"
In my hands, a crown that is yours
For a nation called righteous
A nation called free
A nation that bows
Worship-fully
I will fight
> *I will stand*
O Canada I will stand on guard for thee.[19]

---

[19] This poem came to my heart spontaneously as I was concluding the introduction.

PRELUDE TO THE RESEARCH

So now to the research! I've had my "dusting brush" out and I think I may have found a few foundations that the LORD wants you to see too.

Be encouraged.
Listen with your spirit.
Consider the call.

Compilation disclaimer: This compilation of research is by no means a complete work — there are many other men and women of God and national facts that could have been included. This compilation includes, what I felt, were the most impacting historical facts pertaining to our righteous foundations that I came across while doing research — I believe there is more to be compiled and "dusted" off.

The

RESEARCH

The Righteous
Foundations of Canada

"If the foundations are destroyed,
What can the righteous do?"
(Psalm 11:3)

"And **they shall rebuild** *the old ruins,*
they shall raise up *the former desolations and*
they shall repair *the ruined cities, the*
desolations of many generations...you shall be
named priests of the Lord, **they shall call you the**
servants of our God...*Instead of your shame you*
shall have double honour, and instead of
confusion **they shall rejoice in their portion.**
Therefore in the land **they shall possess double;**
everlasting joy shall be theirs."
(Isaiah 61:4-7)

Bolded text added.

CHAPTER 1
•
A VISION FOR THIS LAND:
Visions in the
Hearts of Canada's First Explorers
and Missionaries & Early Christian
Contact With the First Nations

In the process of "dusting" I was extremely encouraged to discover that many of the first explorers and settlers of Canada received clear mandates, through dreams and visions, to come to the land which would one day be called "The Dominion of Canada." These ones were sent by the voice of God with specific instructions to share Christ with the First Nations and to build a place that would give glory to His name. They had great strength to endure tremendous hardship because of this vision that burned so deeply in their hearts. What an awesome heritage we have!

This chapter outlines many of their stories and words. I believe you will find their lives and walk of faith before the LORD compelling, inspiring and challenging. May we go as they went and give as they gave — for the sake of a nation, for the name of the LORD, for the sake of a generation yet unborn may we fight and may we stand.

FIRST CONTACT
THE VIKINGS

The Viking "Lief Ericsson, converted to Christ in Norway in 1003 AD."[1]

He left "Europe and wintered in Newfoundland in 1004 AD. [Ericsson] was the first known white man to present the gospel of Jesus Christ to Canada's native peoples. An Inuit carving, found on Baffin Island, depicts a Norseman bearing a Christian cross, giving silent testimony to this man's influence 1000 years ago."[2]

JOHN CABOT
(c. Unknown- c.1498)

"...[Landed on Newfoundland's shores claiming it 'For God and for England.' "

"The 'official' discovery of Canada is given to John Cabot who landed on Newfoundland's shores in 1497 claiming it 'For God and for England.' "[3]

JAQUES CARTIER (1491-1557)
French Explorer

"With our hands raised to heaven we yielded our thanks to God."

"In 1533, Jacques Cartier sailed up the St. Lawrence River to Montréal. To commemorate the founding of Montréal, Cartier wrote in his diary... 'we all kneeled down in the company of the Indians and with our hands raised toward heaven yielded our thanks to God.' "[4]

At Hochelaga, "The Hochelagan leader, Agouhanna, who was partially paralyzed, was carried in on a large deerskin and presented to Cartier. [Cartier explained,] 'He showed his arms and legs to me motioning to me to be good enough to

"One would have thought Christ had come down to earth to heal them."

touch them, as if he thereby expected to be cured and healed. On this I set about rubbing his arms and legs with my hands.' Others came to Cartier; the lame, the blind, the elderly and ailing, 'in order that [he] might lay my hands upon them, so that one would have thought Christ had come down to earth to heal them.' Cartier addressed his impromptu assembly, reading from the Gospel of St. John: 'In the beginning was the Word, and the Word was with God and the Word was God.' "[5]

"We who are unworthy, exercise on earth the power of the Lord and seek with all our might to bring those sheep of His flock who are outside into the fold."

"In a letter to France, Cartier exclaimed, 'We who are unworthy, exercise on earth the power of the Lord and seek with all our might to bring those sheep of His flock who are outside into the fold committed to our charge, consider, however, that the Indians are truly men and that they are not only capable of understanding the Catholic Faith but, according to our information, they desire exceedingly to receive it.' "[6]

An Explanation of the Primary Purpose of His Voyage By Cartier:

> *"I am of the opinion that it pleases God in His divine goodness, that all human beings inhabiting the surface of the globe are to have in times to come knowledge and belief in holy faith."*

"I, in my simple understanding and without being able to give any other reason, I am of the opinion that it pleases God in His divine goodness, that all human beings inhabiting the surface of the globe, just as they have sight and knowledge of the sun, have had and are to have in times to come, knowledge and belief in our holy faith."[7]

"His desire to serve the Lord Jesus was also witnessed to by the many episodes of his sharing with the Indian tribes he met; chiefly the reading of the gospel of John, recounting the passion of Jesus and praying for the sick. He also debated with them and questioned them about religion; never fearing to challenge them with the gospel."[8]

SAMUEL DE CHAMPLAIN (1567-1635)

Explorer

Founder of New France

"I should be committing a great sin if I did not make it my business to devise some means of bringing them to the knowledge of God."

*A Diary Entry Regarding the First Nations People
By Champlain:*

They are "living without God and without religion...I thereupon concluded in my private judgement that I should be committing a great sin if I did not make it my business to devise some means of bringing them to the knowledge of God."[9]

"Champlain cared deeply about the First Nations people, building lasting friendships with many groups. Pere Lalemant in 1640 wrote:

> "Champlain cared deeply about the First Nations people, building lasting friendships with many groups."

'Would God that all the French, who were the first to come into these regions, had been like him!' Champlain spoke prophetically to a gathering of the Montagnais, Algonkin, and French: 'Our sons shall wed your daughters and henceforth we shall be one people.' "[10]

"Champlain's relationship with the Indians was an unparalleled success...The Indians, to Champlain, were not exploitable savages but men in need of God and His grace."[11]

"In one of his reports he writes about a conversation he had with an Indian leader in which he stated, 'That God was wholly good; that the sun, moon and stars which they beheld, were created by this great God; that He sent His dear Son, who took on human flesh, worked infinite miracles, raised the dead, healed the sick, cast out devils and taught men the will of God; that He shed His blood for our sins and redeemed mankind...and if they would believe in God as we do, the devil would have no power over them and could do them no harm.' He encouraged European Christians to settle among the Indians and founded Quebec City in 1608."[12]

> "The Indians, to Champlain, were not exploitable savages but men in need of God and His grace."

"To [the First Nations] he was more than a useful ally in wartime. They respected his sense of honour, and long after his death remembered the temperance which marked his conduct when he lived in their villages...despite hardships, disaster and repeated failures, the courage and loyalty of Champlain stood firm. His sincere devotion to his God, his country and his task mark this man as truly one of the brightest of historical figures in the world."[13]

"Looking at Champlain's character, one finds a man of unflinching loyalty, with strength of integrity, and an unselfish servant's heart. Charles W. Colby describes Champlain as follows: 'His narrative abounds throughout with simple and natural expressions of piety...free from trace of the theological intolerance which envenomed French life of his age. And not only did Champlain's trust for the Lord fortify his soul against fear, but religion imposed upon him a degree of self-restraint which was not common among explorers of the seventeenth century."[14]

> *"Looking at Champlain's character, one finds a man of unflinching loyalty, with strength of integrity, and an unselfish servant's heart."*

"Clearly Champlain considered God as his sole protector."[15]

SAMUEL DE CHAMPLAIN (1567-1635) & SIEUR DE PIERRE DU GUA MONTS (SIEUR DE MONTS) (C.1560–C.1630)

Explorer

Founder of New France

Businessman

"Champlain & Sieur de Monts were persevering people of vision and faith who made enormous sacrifices to pioneer this great land of Canada."

"Sieur de Monts was given an exclusive charter by King Henry IV to summon the natives to a knowledge of the Christian religion."

"Champlain & Sieur de Monts were persevering people of vision and faith who made enormous sacrifices to pioneer this great land of Canada."[16]

"In very real terms, Champlain especially helped define who we are as Canadians."[17]

"The man behind Champlain, Sieur de Monts was a French Huguenot businessman who was given an exclusive charter by King Henry IV to summon the natives to a knowledge of the Christian religion."[18]

"Champlain and de Monts, as Fathers of Canada, established their first settlement at St. Croix Island. Both Huguenot (French Protestant) and Roman Catholics were included among the original 79 settlers, along with a Huguenot pastor and a Roman Catholic priest."[19]

Jesuits and the Huron Indians

"'We may be on the point of shedding our blood,' wrote Le Jeune [a Jesuit priest], 'and to sacrifice our lives in the service of our good Master Jesus Christ. It seems that his goodness wants to accept this sacrifice from me.' "[20]

"If [the Lord] should want us to die this very hour, then what a glorious hour it is for us!"

"If [the Lord] should want us to die at this very hour, then what a glorious hour it is for us!"[21]

THEIR MARTYRDOM

"The Iroquois attacked and massacred the Huron...Jesuits Daniel, Jogues, Lalemant, and Brébeuf were taken prisoner, tortured and executed."[22]

80

JEAN DE BRÉBEUF (1593-1649)

First Canadian Martyr
Jesuit Missionary to the Huron

"Jesus Christ was the sole reason for living and, indeed, for dying."

"To Thee my blood, my body and my life!"

"[H]is unbridled commitment to God's work among the Huron resulted in his canonization by Pius XI in 1930 and, in 1940, his being proclaimed the patron saint of Canada by Pius XII."[23]

"Jesus Christ was the sole reason for living and, indeed, for dying, as he reveals in his diary:

> 'My God, my Savior, I take from Thy hand the cup of Thy sufferings. I vow never to fail Thee in the grace of martyrdom, if by Thy mercy, Thou dost offer it to me. I bind myself, and when I have received the stroke of death, I will accept it from Thy gracious hand with all pleasure and with joy in my heart; to Thee my blood, my body and my life!' "[24]

"It is in God alone that my heart rests, and, outside Him, all is naught to me."

"Fifteen years before his death, he told his Huron friends that 'it is in God alone that my heart rests, and, outside Him, all is naught to me.' "[25]

"The Jesuits [saw their mandate to the Huron] as a prototype for native evangelization and a model for other missions."[26]

"In a letter to priests in France who were considering joining the mission, he wrote:

'Your life hangs by a thread. Of calamities you are the cause — the scarcity of game, a fire, famine, or an epidemic...you are the reason, and at any time a savage may burn your cabin down or split your head. Wherein the gain, you ask? There is no gain but this-that what you suffer shall be of God. So if despite these trials you are ready to share our labours, come; for you will find a consolation in the cross that far outweighs its burdens.' "[27]

"So if despite these trials you are ready to share our labours, come; for you will find a consolation in the cross that far outweighs its burdens."

"Father Ragueneau, another of Brébeuf's superiors, is known to have commented, 'I find nothing more frequent in Brébeuf's memoirs than the expression of his desire to die for Jesus Christ.' "[28]

STORY OF JEAN DE BRÉBEUF'S MARTYRDOM

"...Brébeuf's death ranks among the most atrocious martyrdom in the annals of Christianity. The few Huron prisoners who escaped provided Jesuit scribes with eyewitness accounts of how he was killed. The Jesuits later confirmed their stories by examining Brébeuf's body. Brébeuf was stripped naked by the triumphant Iroquois. His fingernails were torn from his fingers, and he was then beaten with sticks and bound to a stake. He exhorted his fellow captives to suffer patiently and promised heaven as their reward. His feet were severed from his legs so that he could not smother the fire that was lit at the base of the stake. Then, as the Iroquois taunted him, boiling water was slowly poured over his head in a mockery of baptism. Still, Brébeuf did not cry out.

> *"It is in his death that his life is best understood and that his work bore its greatest fruit. Conversions, which for many years were few in number, grew in number in the hundreds and even thousands in the years following."*

In a rage, strips of flesh were cut from his limbs, roasted, and devoured before his eyes. Brébeuf, the prized captive of the Iroquois, seemed insensible to pain, further enraging the Iroquois, who took pride in their ability to torture. As he continued to pray aloud, his captors cut away his tongue and lips and thrust a glowing iron shaft down his throat. With the torture entering its fourth hour, Brébeuf was scalped. Seeing him near death, they laid open his breast and devoured his heart and drank his blood, thinking that they might imbibe some portion of his courage...It is in his death that his life is best understood and that his work bore its greatest fruit. Conversions, which for many years were few in number, grew to number in the hundreds and even thousands in the years following Brébeuf's martyrdom. The dispersion of the Huron spread the

Christian faith among the native peoples of the Great Lakes. And these converts formed the Christian communities that the Jesuits were to found among the Iroquois and the natives of the west. Brébeuf's death, like his Savior's, led others to eternal life."[29]

"Brébeuf's death, like his Savior's, led others to eternal life."

MARIE GUYART DE L'INCARNATION (1599-1672)
The Mother of New France

"It was Canada that I showed you. You must go there to build a house for Jesus."

"Commanded by a vision, Marie Guyart – better known as Marie de l'Incarnation – arrived in 1639 in what would become Quebec City. By 1642, Marie, an Ursuline nun, had established the first school and built a convent in New France."[30]

"At age seven, she saw the Lord. 'Do you want to be mine?' He asked."

"Marie was born in 1599 in the French town of Tours into an industrious family of craftsmen and bakers. As a child, she spent hours talking with God and would stand on a chair and repeat sermons that she heard in church. At age seven, she saw the Lord Jesus in what she later described as a mystical dream. 'Do you want to be mine?' He asked. 'Yes,' she replied. Marie's affirmation was to be a lifelong commitment."[31]

"Against her wishes, her parents arranged her marriage at seventeen to a man in whom she had no interest. Two years later, she was a widowed young mother. She discouraged all further suitors, lived with her father, and earned a living as an embroiderer. Although Marie's desire to become a nun remained unabated her worldly affairs kept her from withdrawing into a cloister. She was urged to remarry to reestablish her financial situation, but she chose instead the reading of works of piety and conversing with God."[32]

"In her diary, Marie tells of a unique spiritual experience on the morning of March 25,1620, when an irresistible force descended upon her. In a moment, the eyes of her spirit were opened and all her faults and imperfections were revealed to her with a clearness more certain than any

"An irresistible force descended upon her. In a moment the eyes of her spirit were opened."

certitude. She saw herself immersed in Christ's blood. After confession, she was completely changed, and committed to prayer. She studied the Gospels, meditated on the life of Christ, and practiced the sacraments at her local parish church."[33]

"Her son, Claude, had entered college at age twelve, a separation that was heart-rending for Marie. She sought the advice for her priest and waited for divine guidance. In January 1631, she asked her sister to care for her son and entered the novitiate of the Ursulines of Tours.

"She was obeying divine commands."

Distraught, Claude tried to storm the convent with a band of schoolboys. Amid the uproar, Marie overheard him crying; 'Give me back my mother, give me back my mother.' She would later say of her decision to leave her son that no human explanation can justify such an action, she was obeying divine commands."[34]

"Marie took her vows in 1633 as Marie de l'Incarnation."[35]

"In yet another dream, however, God took her to a vast country full of mountains, valleys, and heavy fogs. 'It was Canada that I showed you, and', the Lord said, 'you must go there to build a house for Jesus'…Marie interpreted the dream to mean that she must go to New France to evangelize the natives and to build a convent and a school."[36]

"In addition, Marie found herself increasingly aligned with Compagnie des Cent-Accociés (the Company of One Hundred Associates), which, already at work in New France, assisted her in getting the bishop of Tours to allow her to pursue her vision. In May 1639, she set sail from Dieppe accompanied by two other Ursuline nuns and one of her main lay supporters, Marie Madeleine de la Peltrie. After three months at sea, they disembarked at the future site of Quebec City, then a community of a few dozen inhabitants. Marie threw herself wholeheartedly into the demands of the

"Marie threw herself wholeheartedly into the demands of the new country, striving to be of service to through teaching native girls and to save souls through sharing the Gospel."

86

new country, striving to be of service through teaching native girls and to save souls through sharing the Gospel."[37]

"Marie's letters overflow with picturesque stories describing the children of the woods, whom she often referred to as the delights of her heart and with whom she recommended that the nuns use affection. Her work among adult Indians was equally passionate. ...She studied Indian languages under the Jesuits and mastered them to such a degree that she wrote Algonquin, Iroquois, Montagnais, and Ouendat dictionaries and a catechism in Iroquois."[38]

"She was dead to herself to such a degree, and Jesus Christ possessed her so completely that one may assuredly say of her, as of the Apostle, that it was not she who lived, but Jesus Christ in her, and that she lived and acted only through Jesus Christ."

"Tenaciously, she disagreed with Quebec's bishop Laval and his attempts to control Quebec's Ursulines. She vigorously opposed him and openly challenged his authority over the religious community. Not until after her death was the bishop of Quebec able to impose his rule on the Ursulines. Bishop Laval, with whom she had sparred for so long, eulogized her. We consider as a special blessing the acquaintance which it pleased God to give us with her...She was dead to herself to such a degree, and Jesus Christ possessed her so completely, that one may assuredly say of her, as of the Apostle, that it was not she who lived, but Jesus Christ in her, and that she lived and acted only through Jesus Christ."[39]

"Marie de l'Incarnation is considered to be one of the greatest of Catholic mystics."[40]

PAUL DE CHOMEDEY DE MAISONNEUVE (1612-1676)

Cofounder of Montréal

"Maisonneuve had 'a desire to make redemption accessible to the native people of New France.' "

Maisonneuve had "a desire to make redemption accessible to the native people of New France...[this desire] led to the creation of Montréal in 1642, with Maisonneuve its first governor."[41]

"Maisonneuve, along with a group of affluent Catholic mystics in France, were moved by visions to build a missionary centre in the wilderness with the intention of converting the natives."[42]

"After stepping out of a boat and putting his feet on the soil [Maisonneuve] dropped to his knees to adore God. They all sang psalms and hymns to the Lord. The purpose of the colony was to 'bring about the glory of God and the salvation of the Indians.'"[43]

"On May 17, 1642, Maisonneuve founded Ville-Marie…Mass was celebrated, and Father Vimont, the superior of the Jesuits in Canada, sermonized: 'You are a grain of mustard seed that shall rise and grow until its branches overshadow the earth. You are few, but your work is the work of God.'"[44]

"A report on Ville-Marie said '…all live in Jesus Christ, with one heart and soul.'"[45]

VILLE MARIE ON THE ISLAND OF MONTRÉAL

"This colony was the product of...Jerome le Toyer de la Dauversier, to whom God has spoken of this mission in a dream....[he] and his wife invested their fortune in this undertaking."[46]

"They invested their fortune in this undertaking...a dream to bring pious natives and Frenchmen together."

"Ville-Marie was born of a dream: to bring pious natives and Frenchmen together to create a new people of God."[47]

THE FLOOD OF 1642

Montréal "was nearly destroyed by a flood in its first winter. On Christmas Eve 1642, the Sainte Lawrence River overflowed. After consulting with the chaplains, Maisonneuve promised that he would carry a cross to the top of Mount Royal if the waters that were already surging against the gates of the fort subsided without causing serious damage. He put his promise in writing; had it read publicly; and then placed a cross, at whose foot was the written statement, on the bank of the overflowing river. After much prayer...the waters subsided. Two weeks later, Maisonneuve carried a cross through the bush to the top of Mount Royal. Today, an illuminated cross marks the spot."[48]

"After much prayer...the waters subsided."

JEANNE MANCE (1606-1673)
Founder of the First Hospital in Montréal

JEANNE MANCE (1606-1673)
Fondatrice de l'Hôtel-Dieu de Montréal
Cofondatrice de la Ville de Montréal
Musée des Hospitalières de l'Hôtel-Dieu

*"God's will is the
only desire and
love of my heart."*

"There is nothing in the world that I would refuse to do to accomplish the divine and all-loving will of God. [God's will] is the only desire and love of my heart. Therein is my passion, all my affections, my only love, and my sole paradise. In a word, it's my God; the will of God is my God. The good pleasure of my God is my God."[49]

SETTLERS OF COURAGE AND FAITH

*"They all believed that
this was a holy war, in
which the glory of God
and the salvation of
souls was at stake."*

"June 1665, two Vessels of Settlers sent by King Louis XIV to New France: 'They all believed they would perish in the storms during the crossing. They [believed]…that this [was] a holy war, in which the glory of God and the salvation of souls [was] at stake.' "[50]

MARGUERITE BOURGEOYS (1620-1700)
Canada's First Schoolmistress

"She left the security of a seventeenth-century French bourgeoisie life to serve the early pioneers in New France."

"'All I have ever desired most deeply and what I still most ardently wish is that the great precept of the love of God above all things, and of thy neighbor as oneself, be written in every heart.' So wrote Marguerite Bourgeoys, who left the security of a seventeenth-century French bourgeoisie life to serve the early pioneers in New France. She assisted in bringing the gospel to the natives, established schools, taught vocational and domestic skills to women, helped the poor, and founded the Congrégation de Notre-Dame de Montréal."[51]

"In 1652, Marguerite met Paul de Chomedey de Maisonneuve, who had founded the settlement of Ville-Marie on the island of Montréal in Canada in 1642 for the express purpose of carrying the gospel to the Amerindians of the New World. Its organizers, a group of devout men and women in France who financed, recruited, and planned the settlement, believed that, just as other Christians had left the

"They believed that they were responsible for reaching the aboriginals of North America with the gospel of Jesus Christ."

Mediterranean world to carry the gospel to their ancestors in northern Europe so they were now responsible for reaching the aboriginal peoples of North America. They hoped to live in a settlement that would reflect that of the early Christian church as described in the Acts of the Apostles."[52].

"In 1658, Marguerite opened Montréal's first school."[53]

"After [young women] married, Marguerite visited them in their homes to teach them to read and to perform for them whatever services were required. Marguerite, who greatly valued the role of women in the family and in society, saw in these women the future of Canada. She welcomed them, helped them adjust to their new conditions, and later supported them in their efforts to raise families."[54]

"Although the transmission of the Christian faith was the most important part of their mission, they also taught reading, writing, arithmetic and the skills needed to earn a living. Because they considered the last such an important responsibility in the teaching of the poor, they even opened

"The transmission of the Christian faith was the most important part of their mission."

a vocational school for the teaching of older women. All of this education was offered free of charge. Marguerite wanted her community to be self-supporting, and her members worked hard not to be a burden to the settlement. They lived a poor and simple life close to the ordinary colonists."[55]

LOUIS DE BUADE DE FRONTENAC (1622-1698)
Governor of Canada
Huguenot

"In 1679, Count Frontenac, a devout Huguenot (French Protestant), and one of the Governors of Canada, declared to the First Assembly, 'As for me, I shall esteem myself happy in consecrating all my efforts, and if need be, my life itself, to extending the Empire of Jesus Christ throughout all this land.' "[56]

B. W. E. CORMACK, NARRATIVE OF A JOURNEY ACROSS THE ISLAND OF NEWFOUNDLAND (in 1822)

B. W. E. Cormack described the First Nations he encountered saying that "their religious ceremonies, of which they are observant, consist of a combination of church and their own primitive ceremonies...by the earliest dawn of day, all join in prayer; and nearly the whole of Sunday."[57]

"All joined in prayer... nearly the whole of Sunday."

They spend all of Sunday "singing hymns."[58]

"They had in their possession a French manuscript of sacred music, given to them they said, by the French Roman Catholic clergyman at the island of St. Peter's."[59]

THE MICMAC CROSS
OF BAY DE NORD

(The Micmac Nation was one of the initial First Nations groups to receive the gospel of Jesus Christ. To date the Micmac prayer book is one of our nation's oldest publications.)

There is a Micmac cross "located on a terrace approximately 150 meters above the sea level. It lies flat on a granite rock surface with the placement of small rocks forming the outline...The cross is believed to be a source of curative and healing powers...The Micmacs contend that they did not construct the cross but rather accidentally discovered it...The cross is still held in high regard by members of the Conne River community."[60]

Left:
Picture of Micmac women

Below:
Micmac Prayer Book

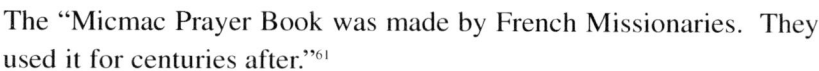

The "Micmac Prayer Book was made by French Missionaries. They used it for centuries after."[61]

96

BISHOP FLEMMING (1792-1850)
VISIT AT CONNE RIVER (in 1834)
Explorer

Bishop Flemming

"Wherever they settle for a season...the first thing they do is to unite, and by their joint labour erect a large wigwam, which they use as a house of prayer."

"Speaking of the Natives he reported '...their piety, the air of recollection they exhibit at their devotions, their attachment to their religion, and their veneration for its ministers, are edifying in the extreme. In rearing their children they are particularly careful to instill into their tender minds a love of purity and attachment to every virtue. Wherever they settle for a season, for they lead a wandering life, the first thing they do is to unite, and by their joint labour erect a large wigwam, which they use as a house of prayer.' "[62]

"They invariably observe the Sabbath with the most scrupulous exactness...On Sundays and holydays of the year they invariably assemble together in the morning, and after singing the *Kyrie Eleison,* the *Gloria,* and *Credo,* they offer the Rosary, and some other prayers, usually occupying an hour; and in the afternoon they meet again and sing Vespers, for they have not only books of devotion written in their own language, but also the principal hymns and psalms set to the Gregorian chant."[63]

ARCHDEACON WIX'S (1802-1866) TRAVELS (in 1835)

Explorer

ARCHDEACON WIX

> **"They certainly are no strangers to prayer...I found, while I myself was among them, that the Indians were very regular in their evening and morning devotions."**

Archdeacon Wix reported regarding his travels, "I met with an interesting Indian [who had] a character of holiness, and a great influence over his tribe,"[64]. as well, "I learned from Maurice Louis, that *Zeul prestoul*, in their language signified 'God save you!' and *a la zeud mat*, 'let us praise God!'...they certainly are no strangers to prayer...and I found, while I was myself among them, that the Indians were very regular in their evening and morning devotions and attention to their rosaries, and that, as the Romanists, they were very particular in carrying their children over to the Romish priest at the French island of St. Peters for baptism. The females particularly had a soft melodious hum in which they chanted with much seeming devotion, every night before they gave themselves to rest."[65]

REVIVAL IN THE ATLANTIC REGIONS

During the 1700's "In Nova Scotia the Holy Spirit was falling profoundly. The French had just been defeated by Britain and the 1776 American War of Independence was about to begin. United Empire Loyalists who sensed what was coming moved North to Canada and settled in Nova Scotia. One of these men, a Baptist minister named Ebenezer Moulton, established the first Baptist Church in Canada. He was followed by a man named Henry Alline. Alline was a Congregationalist with a strong evangelistic ministry emphasizing revival. Hundreds were saved and the entire province awakened to God."[66]

"This revival was called 'The New Light Revival.' It set the foundation for the spread of the gospel in the Atlantic Provinces. New Brunswick felt the impact of revival fires in the early 1800's. Joshua Marsden, a Methodist evangelist, preached in Saint John and it is recorded that 'many of the young people who are subjects of this work, were once loose in their principles and irregular in their practices but they are now new creatures and one can hardly go through the streets of this little city without hearing the voice of praise or seeing the young men assembling together for prayer.' "[67]

RAISING THE DEAD IN KINGSTON

"From its incorporation as a town, there had always been a strong Christian element in Kingston. In 1805, there was an outdoor revival which drew some 2,500 people, when the entire population of Kingston was barely a thousand men, women and children. An eyewitness recorded it as follows: 'A number of evangelists of the Methodist faith have held a camp service which has lasted for several days now. People have come as far as three days' journey just to be here, and oh, what a sight, as they praised God by campfires far into the night! There have been great miracles of healing the sick, and no less, the conversion of countless sinners. Yet there was more – six were raised from the dead!' "[68]

WILLIAM CASE (1780-1855)
Father of Methodist Indian Missions

"I would freely spend
my life among them
for Jesus' sake."

Case, who stated, "'I would freely spend my life among [the First Nations] for Jesus' sake'...volunteered for missionary service in far-off Upper Canada."[69]

Case "realized that indigenous missionaries who understood native culture and spoke native languages must accomplish the mission to native peoples. His role would be that of administrator, coach, and encourager. He would also supervise the translation of scriptures and hymns into native languages."[70]

"During the 1820s and 1830s, over a thousand native converts were baptized [and] many tribal groups requested that teachers be sent to them."[71]

"Case had a sweet singing voice with which he often captivated audiences. He loved the camp meeting songs and the hymns of Charles Wesley. 'The Garden Hymn' became a sort of signature song for him, a verse of which he often used as an invitation:

Amen, amen, my soul replies,
In bound to meet you in the skies,
And claim my mansion there:
Now here is my heart, and here is my hand,
To meet you that heavenly land,
Where we shall part no more."[72]

ELIZA CASE (1796-1887)
Female Missionary and Preacher

"In her career as a committed and energetic teacher and preacher, Eliza became one of the most effective and best-known workers with the native Indians in southern Ontario. In her first years as a missionary, she traveled from mission to mission, supervising Indian women, organizing benevolent societies, and teaching children and adults."[73]

"Eliza became one of the most effective and best know workers with the native Indians in Southern Ontario."

"One of Eliza's main activities was the organization of native women's Dorcas societies to raise money to spread Christianity among the Indians."[74]

"She did not hesitate to proclaim her theology with fervour and eloquence and preached extensively."

"Eliza had a passionate need to share her religious convictions. She was an assertive and forceful woman [who] did not hesitate to proclaim her theology with fervour and eloquence and preached extensively. [She] created a sensation preaching in York and began at least one great religious revival in the area."[75]

101

"The prominent Indian missionary Peter Jones wrote about several of her preaching triumphs, including one occasion at Yellowhead's Island in Lake Simcoe where she caused a mild Pentecost...'the very gates of heaven were opened to our souls, and the spirit of God descended upon our hearts.' Jones saw a footpath appear 'like a blaze of fire,' and the whole camp manifested the presence of God."[76]

> *"The very gates of heaven were opened to our souls, and the spirit of God descended upon our hearts."*

Eliza "was greatly sought after for camp meetings and services in private homes. Letitia recorded the reminiscences of one woman whose doorway had become the pulpit for one of Eliza's sermons. The inside of the house was filled with women, while the men stood in the large yard in front. Eliza's text was from Ezekiel's vision of the waters, and the woman recalled that, 'When the preacher [Eliza] spoke of the spread of the Gospel, and quoted in raptured accents, the waters were still rising...I fancied I could still see the waters of life flowing in until the earth was filled with the glory of God."[77]

> *"The inside of the house was filled with women, while the men stood in the large yard in front."*

> *"On Sundays, there could be as many as six sessions of prayer meetings, preaching, services and classes."*

"In an era when women were considered to be the weaker sex, Eliza tangibly dispelled the notion...Eliza's days began at five o'clock in the morning in winter, at four in the summer. She and other female missionaries were in charge of weekday schools for girls and instructed women in the evening. On Sundays, there could be as many as six sessions of prayer meetings, preaching, services, and classes."[78]

"Eliza had contributed greatly to the spread of Christianity in Canada."

"By the time she died at the age of ninety-one, Eliza had contributed greatly to the spread of Christianity in Canada and the United States. Her faith served as a dynamic model for the women of her era and continues to do so today."[79]

THE NORTH OF CANADA

MORAVIAN MISSIONAIRIES TO THE INUIT

"Evangelism among the Inuit of Canada is found in Labrador. The Moravian missionary, Christian Erhard, sailed from England in 1752 with two other born again brethren. They began ministering to the Eskimo in Labrador and eventually were tragically killed by those they sought to win to Christ. They were followed by Fens Haven, who took up the challenge. By the end of the 18th. century, the gospel was well established in Labrador and the Moravian influence remains today as a tribute to such courageous men of God."[80]

THE WEST OF CANADA

David Thompson (1770-1851)
Explorer and Statesman

"He wanted to reach the Native people of the West with the gospel of Jesus Christ."

"He always carried his Bible with him and read it out loud at every opportunity... Thompson was a pioneer of the faith."

"In 1784, David Thompson, the great map maker, began his work in Canada's West. What motivated this man to endure such hardship? A vision! He wanted to reach the Native people of the West with the gospel of Jesus Christ. He always carried his Bible with him and read it out loud at every opportunity, to voyageurs and to Indians. Long before missionaries penetrated the West, Thompson was a pioneer of the faith. His records recount the services he held and the number of people who gave their lives to Christ."[81]

"David Thompson developed maps from his surveys between 1784 and 1812. Many of his maps are still being used today. Thompson's words give the reason he endured the physical hardship of exploration: [It was] 'so that these physically impenetrable barriers may be traversed and the Gospel be spread.' "[82]

OTHERS FOLLOW
THOMPSON'S TRAIL

"One century later 'The Salvation Army' followed the same routes that David Thompson mapped out. They formed the Mountaineer Brigade with 40 volunteers spending all their time on horseback, riding the Rockies with the message of the gospel. With the development of the Hudson's Bay Company, the need arose for increased Christian witness. The Governor instructed his officials in Victoria to have regular times of public prayer and scripture readings."[83]

HENRY BIRD STEINHAUER
(1818-1884)
First Nations, Ojibwa
Preacher

Glenbow Archives NA-352-4

"Perhaps none was more dedicated to his work, to his people, and to his God than Henry Bird Steinhauer."

"Early in the nineteenth century, the Methodists in Upper Canada worked extensively among the native people. Mission schools were established 'to win souls for God.' One of the Methodists' highest priorities was to train native leaders who would then minister to their own people. They had many successes, but perhaps none was more devoted to his work, to his people, and to his God than Henry Bird Steinhauer."[84]

"Steinhauer excelled in languages and as a missionary to the Canadian west. [He] actually prepared his sermons from the original Greek texts of the New Testament."[85]

"He set out to translate major portions of the Scripture... into the Cree syllabic system."

"In 1840, the Hudson's Bay Company asked the British Wesleyan Methodist Society to 'minister to the religious and educational needs of the Indians in the Hudson Bay Territories.' Steinhauer answered the call and traveled to the northern tip of Lake Winnipeg, arriving at Norway House in 1843 and taking charge of the school at nearby Rossville. Because of his belief that students should be taught in their own language, Steinhauer's first goal was to learn the Swampy Cree language. Upon accomplishing this, he set out to translate major portions of the Scripture, from Psalms to the end of the Old Testament and from Romans to the end of the New Testament, into the Cree syllabic system."[86]

"Daily devotions were an integral part of life."

"He worked to make the Bible relevant to the Cree, comparing their way of life with that of the early Jews — wandering tribes who lived in tents."[87]

"Even on the hunts, and in spite of threat of attack from other tribes, daily devotions were an integral part of life.

On Sundays, there were four services and an adult Bible study. The celebrations of the 'love-feast' — with the sacrament of communion — were emotional events in which individuals gave testimony of God's effect in their lives. Steinhauer further ensured the well-being of his mission by discouraging traders from establishing trading posts in the area to reduce the influx of alcohol."[88]

"Individuals gave testimony of God's effect in their lives."

"His faith never wavered... His influence lived on."

"Throughout his life, Steinhauer faced many obstacles — starvation, deaths of several children, tribal war, and smallpox epidemics — yet his faith never wavered. He died on December 29th, 1884, but his influence lived on. When rebellion broke out the following year, an Indian chief who did not involve his tribe explained that he chose not to go to war as a tribute to his friend, the man of God who taught peace."[89]

ROBERT RUNDLE (1811-1896)
Missionary

"Like so many other settlements, Fort Edmonton started off as a Hudson's Bay Post, and a few years after its establishment, a missionary named Robert Rundle arrived in 1840. Happily for history he kept a diary. 'March 25 – met with the Indians again. This morning we discussed the resurrection of Jesus, and this afternoon the nature of salvation. How eagerly they listen! My heart was warmed while telling them the blessed truth of the Gospel. Tonight I wrote a verse for the first time in Cree.' "[90]

"Here was an excerpt from a letter to his superiors: 'Oh, I do beg the secretaries to send more missionaries here! What can I do in such an immense field? And will you implore them to send them at once? I want to take the place by storm. I would that my means were adequate to my wishes, but blessed be God! The standard of the Cross is uplifted, and the tribes are flocking to it – is anything too hard for the Lord?' "[91]

"The standard of the Cross is uplifted, and the tribes are flocking to it – is anything too hard for the Lord?"

"I met with the Assiniboine Indians this morning and afternoon. Subject: Jesus Christ. I was delighted to witness their attention. How eagerly they listen to the word of life!"

"In 1841, Robert Rundle left his base of operations, Fort Edmonton, and made the trip to Elbow River, recording in his diary: 'I met with the Assiniboine Indians this morning and afternoon. Subject: Jesus Christ. I was delighted to witness their attention. How eagerly they listen to the word of life! May the Great Shepherd call them to His fold.' Rundle spent his first Easter in western Canada with the Cree and the Assiniboine, whom he taught to sing 'Come to Jesus,' each in their own language. 'The two tribes can now sing it alternately,' he wrote, 'but the most striking part is when they all join in the chorus, *Hallelujah, Amen.* They make the air ring with their melody.' "[92]

"In 1861, Missionary George MacDougall found the Stony Indians still adhering to the Gospel message that had been preached to them by Rundle, twenty years before. And the Cree were freely using the written language invented for them by James Evans and taught them by Rundle...How much more bitter would have been the opening of out west in Canada, had it not been for the sacrificial love of these servants of God?"[93]

Cree syllabic system set up by Methodist missionary James Evans.

108

FATHER ALBERT LACOMBE (1827-1916)
Missionary

Father Albert Lacombe with Blackfoot chiefs Crowfoot, left, and Three Bulls in 1886.

"Twelve years would pass before God sent another labourer to toil in that vineyard [i.e. where Robert Rundle had laboured in the Edmonton area]. He was Father Albert LaCombe, and though only 25 yrs old, he had a remarkable gift for making peace. His dealings with the western Indians, the politicians in Ottawa, and the railroad barons of the Canadian Pacific made him one of Canada's first ambassadors of good will. One day a great warrior brave named Sweetgrass came to Father LaCombe with a gravely wounded son-in-law. The young man had had his hand cut off after an accident with a rifle, but now gangrene had set in and threatened to take his life. 'What can I do?' Father LaCombe asked. 'If he were a Christian, you would certainly do something for him,' Sweetgrass challenged him. 'But for us, you will do nothing.' Father LaCombe accepted the challenge. Praying mightily for God's help, he made a deep incision

"Today in the presence of the [G]reat Spirit, I turn away from all the beliefs of our fathers to follow these of our friend, 'The man of Prayer.'

into the infected area and cleansed the wound as best he could. Three weeks later, much to his surprise, the two returned, and the young brave was completely healed. A short time later, at a meeting that Father LaCombe was having for the Indians, Sweetgrass rose to his feet, and all the others fell silent. 'You all know who I am. You have seen me presiding at the great medicine feasts. Today in the presence of the [G]reat Spirit, I turn away from all the beliefs of our fathers to follow these of our friend, 'The man of Prayer.' '"[94]

DAVID MAINSE AND
REVERND ELWOOD MCCLEAN
Dialogue Regarding the First Nations in the Prairies

Eldwood said, "…The earliest missionaries found that there were certain Indians – and they were in the minority – who said, 'We don't bother with those things, [referring to traditional, non-Christian, First Nations' spirituality]; we won't take part in them.' They refused to make sacrifices of any kind, to any image whatsoever, and they said this: 'I only worship God in my heart.' He paused and looked a bit sad. 'You know a lot of the younger generation among the Indians don't realize that some of their forefathers believed that way. Those men had a revelation of God, an understanding of Him, and I have always said that I have not yet found an Indian atheist.' '"[95]

"The moment that they heard that the Great Spirit had a son named Jesus, who made the supreme and final, complete sacrifice – they said, 'That's it!' "

"These people – and there were many of them who said that they just believed in the Great Spirit in their heart – the moment that they heard that the Great Spirit had a son named Jesus, who made the supreme and final, complete sacrifice – they said, 'That's it!' And they believed immediately, according to the stories of early missionaries, who were bringing the Gospel for the first time."[96]

FATHER CHARLES PANDOSY

Missionary in Southern British Columbia
Father of the Okanagan

*"He served
Indians
and white
settlers alike."*

Father Charles Pandosy was an "Oblate missionary who came to the system of valleys known as the Okanagan, in 1858. A huge powerfully built man, Father Pandosy had had a vision of endless apple trees, and he began to plant the seeds, as soon as he arrived. Working in poverty, barefoot and bareheaded, he served Indians and white settlers alike as a teacher, doctor, lawyer, botanist, and musician. Other missionaries and many more settlers came to the Okanagan, but Father Pandosy was the outstanding figure among them."[97]

*"Other missionaries
and many more
settlers came to
the Okanagan, but
Father Pandosy
was the
outstanding figure
among them."*

"Thirty-three years after his arrival, Father Pandosy, then 76 and no longer in robust health, typically embarked on a long winter canoe trip to bear the light of Christ further inland. He took sick and died in the arms of an old Indian friend, and when his body was returned in state for burial at his mission, he was mourned by all the settlers and Indians, and referred to as the Father of the Okanagan."[98]

WILLIAM DUNCAN (1832-1918)

Missionary to the First Nations in
Northern British Columbia

"He was an exemplary man and one of the most biblical messengers among the First Nations."

William Duncan was a missionary to the Tshimpshian people in the Port Simpson, Pr. Rupert, and Metlakatla areas. He was an exemplary man and one of the most biblical messengers among the First Nations.

He stood up against both the Government of Canada, Hudson Bay Co., and then also the Anglican Church in order to bring the pure message of the Gospel to the people. He also worked to establish the Gospel among the Tsimpshians in a way that would elevate them as a people and position them for the inevitable, encroaching, European presence. Duncan was so successful in establishing a self-governing and prospering community that, at one point, the white settlers had to come to the Tsimpshian community to buy from them!

In his work he ran into much resistance from the Government so he petitioned for land in Alaska and received the land which is now

Metlakatka, Alaska. He took a sizeable group of First Nations to this land and there they thrived.

Duncan insisted on biblical principles for the community. Even to this day he is referred as the Lord's "sent one" among the Tsimpshians.

Because of his skill as a musician he became one of the first evangelists on the coast and had choirs and brass bands, which played as far away as San Francisco.

Duncan influenced many First Nations leaders, some of whom put an end to all their spirit-rooted feasts. At one point most of the village of Old Kitselas was born again.[99]

"Duncan influenced many First Nations leaders, some of whom put an end to all the spirit-rooted feasts. At one point most of the village of Old Kitselas was born again."

HISTORICAL OVERVIEW OF OUR CANADIAN CHRISTIAN HERITAGE
BY ANNE COLEMAN

"In 1497, John Cabot planted a cross on the shores of Newfoundland. It was the first to be discovered by the Vikings and the last province to enter Confederation. It has as its motto, 'Seek first the Kingdom of God.' Next to be explored — New France, now the provinces of Quebec, New Brunswick and Nova Scotia. Jacques Cartier planted and raised at least two crosses from 1534-1535. The motto for Quebec is 'I remember.' God commands us to remember and to tell His deeds to the coming generations. Cartier, when met by the Indians near the St. Lawrence River at Montréal, read from the Gospel of St. John and prayed for the sick to be healed.

"John Cabot planted a cross on the shores of Newfoundland... [the province] has as its motto 'Seek first the Kingdom of God.'"

At the founding of Montréal in May 1642, three hundred and fifty years ago, a Thanksgiving Service was held. The prophetic speech by Father Vimont was given: 'You are a grain of mustard seed that shall rise and grow till its branches overshadow the earth. You are few; but your work is the work of God. His smile is on you and your children shall fill the land.' The founder of Montréal, Paul de Chomedy, Sieur de Maisonneuve quoted to his own father: 'There is no man that hath left house or brethren, sister, or fathers for my sake but he shall receive a hundred-fold.' When Montréal was

"At the founding of Montreal the prophetic speech by Father Vimont was given: 'You are a grain of mustard seed that shall rise and grow till its branches overshadow the earth...His smile is on you and your children shall fill the land.'"

preserved from destruction, he carried a cross to the top of Mount Royal. A lighted cross stands there today, two hundred and fifty years later. Montréal was settled in an area of peace, a 'no man's land' among the Indians. Peace, prosperity and healing is to come from this cradle and birthplace…A plaque placed on the gates of the memorial and burial place of the United Empire Loyalists at Adolphustown, Ontario quotes Exodus 3:5, 'Take off your sandals for the place you stand is holy ground.' God's hand has continued to guide Canada's development. During the American Revolution when George Washington was pressed by the people to invade Canada, he wrote on August 11th, 1775 that '…such an enterprise is inconsistent with the General Principal upon which the colonies have proceeded, since defense, not conquest was their objective.'…July 1st, 1811 the famous Methodist bishop Frances Ashbury finally achieved a lifelong desire to visit Canada. Upon crossing the St. Lawrence River into Canada, he exclaimed, 'this is the land that God has blessed.' He was very instrumental in sending the 'circuit riders' with the gospel into Canada. A plaque in Charlottetown refers to the Fathers of Confederation 'Providence being their guide, they builded better than they knew'[20] …The national anthem, 'O Canada'[21] was originally written in French in the 1880's. The vision is very clearly stated there: 'Because your arm is able to carry the sword. It can also carry the cross! Your history is the epic of the most brilliant exploits: And your bravery tempered with faith, will protect our households and our rights. Under the eyes of God, near a great river the Canadian grew in hope. He was born of a proud race blessed was his cradle. Heaven has blessed his life in this New World. Always guided by its light, he maintains the honour of his

"Upon crossing the St. Lawrence River into Canada, the famous Methodist bishop Frances Ashbury exclaimed, 'this is the land that God has blessed.' "

---

[20] See Chapter 2.

[21] See Chapter 4.

115

flag.' The vision of God using Canada to bring peace, hope and healing to the nations is being restored and proclaimed once again. Dr. Paul Yonggi Cho, Seoul, S. Korea prophesied in Kelowna, B.C., October 31, 1975... *'You have the welcome open door like the open door of Philadelphia church in the Revelation, and you have the finances, and the personnel well-trained; you have the good church, and God calls YOU to rise up to meet this challenge before Christ comes. Clear-cut clarion trumpet sound is coming to Canada!! RISE UP, Canada! Meet the Challenge! God wants YOUR young men and young women to rise up and give their lives as living sacrifices!...I stand here as a 'regained bread', and I now relay God's message to YOU! God is depending upon YOU!'*...This was repeated on August 10, 1984 in Sackville, Nova Scotia. *'...God is going to bless Canada, and the Canadian church is going to rise up once again and go to the four corners of the world and bring the Gospel of Jesus Christ to pave the way for the second coming.'* "[100]

CHAPTER 2:

•

CANADA'S FOUNDERS:
Quotes from
Founding Fathers of Canada and Other
Influential Persons
of the Dominion

Following are quotes from Canada's Founding Fathers and influential leaders of the Dominion in the years of, and following, Confederation. These men and women worked to lay the foundations of Canada. Psalm 89:14 declares, "Righteousness and justice are the foundation of [His] throne." As discussed in the introduction, the good news for us as Canadians is that at the birth of our nation there were many righteous foundations laid! The purpose of this section is to highlight these Godly foundations so that we can pull them forth and reestablish them in our generation (see the Prophetic Introduction, specifically, the section on the "Agreement of the Ages").

*Psalm 11:3b says, "If the foundations are destroyed what can the righteous do?" Some translations say, "What **will** the righteous **do**?" (emphasis added). In many ways a survey of the nation of Canada today leads one to wonder what has happened to the original intentions of the fathers of the land. Again, as presented in the introduction, I believe the substance of these intentions are still here. I believe the LORD is saying that they are lying dormant in the fabric of the nation and that He is just waiting for a generation to call them forth and reestablish them for today. What **will** the righteous in this generation **do**?*

In response to this righteous history, may we rise up in the spirit of King Josiah who, after discovering the Law that the LORD had given to Moses, dedicated his efforts during his reign to tearing down the idols of foreign gods and reestablishing the nation in righteousness. Now it is our turn! Let's run our leg with zeal, excellence, undivided focus and grace!

Prayer:

O God hear, O God renew, O God restore by Your Spirit and grace. God heal our land and raise up the age old foundations — through our hands (Isaiah 61:4).

SIR SAMUEL LEONARD TILLEY (1818-1896)

Premier of New Brunswick
Father of Confederation

"When reading verse eight of Psalm 72, 'He shall have Dominion also from sea to sea,' the thought occurred to him, 'What a splendid name to give Canada.' "

"Sir Samuel Leonard Tilley, then Premier of NB, was one of the 33 Father's of Confederation. He was a born-again Christian who always started his day with prayer and a chapter of the Bible."[101]

"When the Fathers of Confederation were assembled discussing the terms and conditions of Confederation and the drafting of the British North America Act there had been considerable discussion the day before and many suggestions as to what the new United Canada should be called, and no conclusion had been reached. The discussion on the name stood over until the next day. The next morning, as was Sir Leonard's custom, he read a chapter from the Bible, and that particular morning he read Psalm seventy-two. When reading verse eight of the Psalm, 'He shall have Dominion also from sea to sea,' the thought occurred to him, 'What a splendid name to give Canada.'

When he went back to the sitting of the convention that morning he suggested the word Dominion, which was agreed to, and Canada was called the Dominion of Canada. A letter signed by John A. Macdonald explained to Queen Victoria that the name was a tribute to the principles they earnestly desired to uphold."[102]

"...[O]n [Tilley's] tombstone it was written 'His trust was in Jesus.' "[103]

GEORGE BROWN (1818-1880)

Father of Confederation

Founder of Toronto Globe & Mail

"Let us gratefully acknowledge the hand of the Almighty Disposer of Events in bringing about this result."

Toronto Globe & Mail, July 1st, 1867
By George Brown

"With the first dawn of this gladsome midsummer morn, we hail the birthday of a new nationality. [Canada], with its four million people, takes its place this day among the nations of the world...Old things have passed away...divisions of Upper and Lower, East and West has been completed, and this day a new volume is opened...Let us gratefully acknowledge the hand of the Almighty Disposer of Events in bringing about this result, pregnant with so important an influence on the condition and destinies of the inhabitants of these Provinces, and of the teeming millions who in ages to come will people the Dominion of Canada from ocean to ocean."[104]

CONFEDERATION PORTRAIT

"Nobody can argue with the 'supremacy of God' being recognized as the historic founding principle of Canada."

"Nobody can argue with the 'supremacy of God' being recognized as the historic founding principle of Canada. The picture of the founding fathers of Confederation who chose the title 'Dominion of Canada' as the official name for the new nation-state based on Psalm 72:8 has this caption underneath it, 'Providence being their Guide, they built better than they knew!' "[105]

"Providence being their Guide, they built better than they knew!"

CONVENTION AT CHARLOTTETOWN, PRINCE EDWARD ISLAND.

BISHOP JOHN STRACHAN (1778-1867)
First Anglican Bishop of Toronto
Founder of Ontario's School System

*"You cannot
divorce
religion from
education."*

"Bishop John Strachan, a leader who helped form our public education system, stated that the Church must continue to play a central role in education. 'You cannot divorce religion from education because schools will inevitably reflect the philosophical and religious or (irreligious) biases of those who direct them.' "[106]

EGERTON RYERSON (1803-1882)

Prominent Methodist Minister

Founder of Public Education in Ontario

"Ryerson believed that his primary task was 'to make men Christians.' "

"Ryerson believed that his primary task was 'to make men Christians – Christians in heart and life, in temper and work.' "[107]

He was the "Father of public education in Canada, [and] wanted a common patriotic ground [in the education system] of comprehensiveness and avowed Christian principles."[108]

"Youth should be furnished with right principles as well as right knowledge."

"In 1841, he became the first principal of Victoria College in Coburg. In his inaugural address, he stressed that the college would have a balanced curriculum, infused with the 'fundamental principles of Christian theology.' Ryerson further stated that 'youth should be furnished with right *principles*, as well as with right *knowledge*...the *first* requisite is the religious and moral knowledge of right and wrong: the next is the acquaintance with the history of mankind.' "[109]

"The Ontario school system was to be a Christian Public school system."

"He wrote the textbook 'First Lessons in Christian Morals.' Ryerson clearly said that the Ontario school system was to be a Christian public school system."[110]

"Many of our greatest Canadian universities were founded as denominational seminaries to educate future church leaders."[111]

1896 Public School Act

"The Ontario Public School Act of 1896 stated that 'it shall be the duty of every teacher of a public school to teach diligently and faithfully all of the subjects in the public school...to maintain proper order and discipline in his pupils in his school; to encourage his pupils in the pursuit of learning; to include, by precept and example, respect for religion and the principles of Christian morality and the highest regard for truth, justice, love of country, humanity, benevolence, sobriety, industry, frugality, purity, temperance and all other virtues.' "[112]

"It shall be the duty of every teacher of a public school to teach diligently and faithfully...respect for religion and the principles of Christian morality."

SIR SANFORD FLEMING (1827-1915)
Inventor of Standard Time
Railway Engineer

"I have always felt that the humblest among us has it in his power to do something for his country."

"...I have always felt that the humblest among us has it in his power to do something for his country by doing his duty, and that there is no better inheritance to leave his children than the knowledge that he has done so to the utmost of his ability."[113]

> *"The great objective of education is the development of the human faculties, by the operation of such influence that will subdue our evil natures [and] strengthen our best natures."*

"It will be conceded that the great objective of education is the development of the human faculties, by the operation of such influence that will subdue our evil natures, and will strengthen our best natures, and will cultivate to enrich the mind, so as to form the best possible individual characters. Its grand aim is to ennoble the propensities and tastes, to strengthen the moral sense and to fit man to discharge his duties as an intelligent being, in the best manner in which he is capable in the land in which he lives, and in the age in which he is capable in the land in which he lives, and in the age in which God has given him life…that he may be prepared well to perform his part in elevating the condition of his race, and in raising the character of his country in the scale of nations."[114]

LOUIS RIEL (1844-1885)

Founder of Manitoba
Righteous Reformer
Métis

*"My life belongs to God.
Let Him do what
He wishes with it."*

*"Lord Jesus I love you.
I love everything
associated with you."*

"Riel was very Christ-centered, praying in his diary:
'Lord Jesus, I love you. I love everything associated with You.' "[115]

*"Louis Riel had
a very sensitive,
passionate spirit."*

"'The first time I received the Holy Eucharist, I was trembling,' said Louis Riel. Born at St. Boniface (Winnipeg) on October 22nd 1844, young Louis Riel had a very sensitive, passionate spirit with zero tolerance for bullying. According to Mousseau, 'nothing irritated him as much as an abuse of strength against the weak.' Riel also had a deep life of prayer and fasting, commenting in his diary: 'Fasting and prayer are the two great keys to success in time and eternity…Nothing can resist fasting when it is done with

*"Riel had a deep
life of prayer
and fasting."*

humility, sincerity and devotion. Fasting opens prisons and releases the most hardened criminals...Three or four days of fasting can accomplish more than an army on the field of battle.' "[116]

"God has everything in His care. Have confidence in Jesus Christ."

"In his diary, Riel commented: 'Men can struggle as they will against the will of God and oppose its fulfillment, but they never succeed in excluding it from the guidance of human affairs. God has everything in His care. Have confidence in Jesus Christ.' "[117]

"Writing to his good friend Bishop Tache on Sept 9th 1870, Riel said: 'My life belongs to God. Let him do what He wishes with it.' "[118]

"Riel began to move more in the prophetic, sometimes experiencing intense joy and deep sorrow in church services. With a great effort, Riel tried to suppress his weeping: 'My pain was as intense as my joy.'

"The Spirit of God affects us where He wishes, and to the extent that suits Him."

In Riel's diary, he memorably said: 'The Spirit of God penetrated my brain as soon as I fell asleep...The Spirit of God affects us where He wishes, and to the extent that suits Him.' "[119]

The Birth of Manitoba

"When Riel stood up for the rights of the Métis, he woke up our sleepy Canada nation. After taking over the Hudson Bay Company's Fort Garry, Riel successfully forced Prime Minister Macdonald to recognize Métis land rights, and to accept Manitoba into Confederation as a full Province, and not just another territory. Riel stated to the Federal negotiator Donald Smith: 'We want only our just rights as British subjects, and we want the English to join us simply

132

to obtain these.' On May 12, 1870, the Manitoba Act, based on the Métis 'List of Rights', was passed by the Canadian Parliament."[120]

"Jesus, author of life! Sustain us in all the battles of this life and, on our last day, give us eternal life."

"Before Riel died, he passionately prayed in his diary: 'Jesus, author of life! Sustain us in all the battles of this life and, on our last day, give us eternal life. Jesus, give me the grace to really know your beauty! Grant me the grace to really love You. Jesus, grant me the grace to know how beautiful You are; grant me the grace to cherish You.' "[121]

"Jesus, give me the grace to really know your beauty."

DIALOGUE BETWEEN DAVID MAINSE AND WALTER DINSDALE REGARDING MANITOBA'S NAME:

Walter Dinsdale speaking:
"Manitoba comes from the Indian word *Manitou,* and means 'the dwelling place of the Great Spirit.' And as I look back over thirty years on Parliament Hill, we are now facing a time when it can't be done by politics. Reconciliation cannot be achieved by politics. "It's not by might, nor by power, but by my Spirit saith the Lord." Man proposes,' he concluded, with a twinkle in his eye, 'but, thank goodness, God disposes!' "[122]

WILLIAM HOWLAND (1844-1893)

Businessman
Mayor of Toronto

"Howland was elected mayor on a platform of righteousness saying, 'Let us keep the city, a God-fearing city, and I would rather see it thus than the greatest and richest city in the continent.' "

"By twenty-nine he was the youngest insurance company president in Canada. He was one of Toronto's leading young business executives and served as the president of the Toronto Board of Trade and later as a spokesperson for the Ontario Manufacturer's Association."[123]

"Howland began to channel the ability and energy that had led him to prominence in the business community into work among the needy. It is safe to say that Howland had a part in virtually every philanthropic and relief enterprise in the Toronto of that time. Howland worked hard on behalf of the poor – particularly children – in the lower St. John's ward of Toronto, the most impoverished part of town. His experiences there transformed his perceptions of humanity. He learned of the evils of alcohol abuse. He discovered that the under classes of Toronto did not feel welcome in the city's fine churches. Not one to just observe a problem, Howland was also a man of purpose. He founded the Toronto Mission Union, which ministered to the needs of the poor, the hungry, and the abused through its inner-city mission centres. He also

"Howland began to channel the ability and energy that had lead him to prominence in the business community into work among the needy."

founded the Christian Missionary Union, an evangelistic effort that sought to reach those Torontonians who would not normally attend the city's more traditional churches. In late 1885, a group of reformers in Toronto, made up of prohibitionists, union leaders, and those concerned about the poor, urged Howland to run for mayor. Although winning seemed impossible, he ran as an independent against the Tory party machine. Helped by the vote of landowning women – voting for the first time in a municipal election – Howland won a surprisingly easy victory."[124]

"William Holmes Howland was elected mayor [of Toronto in 1886] on a platform of righteousness. Throughout the campaign, Howland urged voters, Let us keep the city, a God-fearing city, and I would rather see it thus than the greatest and richest city in the continent."[125]

"Not one to just observe a problem, Howland was a man of purpose."

"Howland put a twelve-foot banner on his office wall: Except the Lord keep the city, the watchmen waketh but in vain (Psalm 127:1). This was to be his guiding light."[126]

"'Except the Lord keep the city, the watchmen waketh but in vain.' (Ps. 127:1) This was to be his guiding light."

"He began by enforcing tough rules in the areas of sanitation and public health. He instituted regulations requiring the cleanup of lands used for slaughterhouses and factories...and significant

> *"Howland challenged the large monopolies and business cartels that dealt with the city, forcing them to become responsible in their dealings."*

attempts were made to supply safe drinking water to a rapidly expanding city. He also encouraged the development of suburbs so that working-class people could get out of the squalor and pollution of the inner city. In addition, Howland challenged the large monopolies and business cartels that dealt with the city, forcing them to become responsible in their business dealings. He supported the employees of the Toronto Street Railway when their unreasonable and powerful employer locked them out. And through a judicial commission Howland was able to end the monopoly that an elite group of Toronto coal merchants had enjoyed for years by prosecuting city employees and coal merchants for kickbacks and for the embezzlement of city funds."[127]

> *"With Howland's election, a new type of mayoralty was born, a mayoralty for the whole city."*

"Through Howland's reform in the area of public morality, Toronto received its well known nickname, Toronto the Good. Staff Inspector David Archibald was appointed by Howland to head a special police squad whose task was to 'combat cruelty to animals, women, and children, and to oppose gambling, prostitution, Sabbath-breaking, and unlicensed drinking.' This unique squad initiated the closure of brothels, prosecuted the operators of illegal drinking establishments, and reduced by a third the number of licensed saloons. It also introduced programs to curb the abuse of women and children. These were tangible manifestations of Howland's desire to serve the people of Toronto. Howland, though, did not stop here. He managed, against old-guard resistance, to launch public works for the unemployed and to interest investors in good working-class housing, and he

136

personally spearheaded the drive to create the Mimico Reformatory for Boys, re-moving youngsters from the horrors of the Don Jail."[128]

"With Howland's election, a new type of mayoralty was born, a mayoralty for the whole city. After Howland, the mayors of Toronto were expected to have a vision for the entire city."[129]

"Howland was further eulogized as someone who chose the more lowly, and more Christ-like place of feeding the hungry, visiting the sick, going amongst the hospitals and the prisons, and following in the very steps of the Lord himself."[130]

"Howland was further eulogized as someone who chose the more lowly, and more Christ-like place."

OLIVER MOWAT (1820-1903)

Lawyer
Father of Confederation
Judge
Premier of Ontario
Lieutenant Governor of Ontario

"He declared he would do his duty in Parliament in the spirit and with the views which become a Christian politician."

"As a youth, Oliver Mowat studied the evidence of Christianity very earnestly...and came to the conclusion that Christianity was no cunningly devised fable, but was very truth."[131]

"In standing for federal election in 1857…he declared that if elected he would do his duty in Parliament in the spirit and with the views which become a Christian politician."[132]

"He has been credited with putting the resolutions of the Quebec Conference, which eventually formed the British North America Act of 1867 and gave birth to a new nation, into 'constitutional and legal shape.' "[133]

"He served as the premier and the attorney general of Ontario from 1872 until 1895. His return to political life brought accolades from the press: 'Mr. Mowat will no doubt prove acceptable to all parties. He stands very high as a Christian gentleman.' "[134]

"He stands very high as a Christian gentleman."

"Mowat displayed a sense of social justice that sprang from his Christian convictions which, in turn, manifested themselves in his various affiliations" (i.e. Director, and then Vice President, of the Upper Canada Bible Society, Director of the Anti-Slavery Society of Canada and President of the Evangelical Alliance).[135]

"[H]e studied theology and wrote apologetic works on the life and nature of Jesus Christ. His publications include *Christianity and Some of Its Evidences*, a compilation of statements concerning Christianity's validity and conclusions that can be drawn from the life and miracles of Christ, particularly His resurrection from the dead. Mowat also wrote *Christianity and Its Influence,* which began as a guest lecture to medical students. In his writings, he held to a solidly orthodox but not denominationally narrow creed."[136]

"Mowat displayed a sense of social justice that sprang from his Christian convictions."

> *"He owned himself
> a humble follower
> of Jesus Christ;
> enduring hardness
> for His sake
> as a good soldier."*

"He owned himself a humble follower of Jesus Christ; enduring hardness for His sake as a good soldier, disciplining his moral nature, revering the Sabbath, haunting the sanctuary, studious of God's Word, observed of all as a man of faith and prayer, ever giving to Caesar the things that are Caesar's and to God that things that are God's."[137]

TIMOTHY EATON (1834-1907)
Businessman

> *"He learned
> that the
> honesty
> taught him by
> his mother
> was the best
> policy for
> a merchant."*

"Eaton left school at the age of eighteen and was apprenticed to a dry goods merchant. He slept under the store's counter – convenient for someone who had to work form early morning to late at night six days a week. During his apprenticeship, he learned much about the business of buying and selling and that the honesty taught him by his mother was the best policy for a merchant. In addition, he learned empathy for all who worked long hours for little reward. When his apprenticeship expired, he received only one hundred pounds sterling for five years' work."[138]

"Eaton was revered for his inflexible integrity." "During an open-air meeting, he heard a Methodist minister preaching the Gospel. When an opportunity was given for corporate prayer, Eaton withdrew to a barn to debate with and seek the assistance of God in solitary prayer. On his return to the meeting, he made a confession of faith and soon joined the Methodist Church. In 1861, Eaton met Margaret Beattie while attending St. Mary's Methodist Church. Within weeks, he had proposed, and the couple was soon married. In 1869, they and their three children moved to Toronto, where they purchased a dry goods business on the corner of Queen and Yonge Streets for $6,500. Thus was born the T. Eaton Co. of Toronto, launching a revolution in Canadian retailing."[139]

"Eaton was revered for his inflexible integrity. He mandated that in all advertisements the exact truth should be told with regard to the goods offered for sale. He decreed that if a customer was not satisfied, the price should be refunded. And he remained an unwavering Methodist who never sold tobacco, liquor, or playing cards in his store and did not allow them in his home."[140]

"He lead the country in introducing shorter and [more humane] working hours [for employees] and paid welfare pensions before most employers had even heard the terms."

"During his career, Eaton never forgot the principles that had guided him since his youth. The passing years merely reinforced his reputation for fair dealing. He often urged his sales staff to use no deception in the smallest degree-nothing you cannot defend before God or Man. And he always remembered the long hours of his apprenticeship in Ireland and decided that none of his staff would experience a similar fate. He led the country in introducing shorter working hours and paid welfare and pensions before most employers had even heard the terms. At a time when most Toronto stores

140

remained open until 10:00 p.m., Eaton ran advertisements suggesting to his customers that they shop during the day to 'Liberate Your Fellow-Beings.' "[141]

"Eaton's business boomed, and he moved into constantly larger buildings. By the 1880s, he was among Toronto's leading merchants. He demonstrated his largesse in 1889 as one of the chief founders of Trinity Methodist Church. The Methodist churches on Bloor Street and Robert Street were also built through Eaton's generosity, and he was an important benefactor to the denomination's Victoria College."[142]

"Despite his fame, Eaton preferred to remain largely in the background; he never became a public figure, and he refused to enter politics. He had three principal interests: his church, his family, and his store."[143]

"A man who in matters of faith had the beautiful simplicity of a child and who endeavored to have the Sermon on the Mount wrought out in his daily life."

"At the funeral service in Eaton's home, the Reverend Joseph Odery mourned the loss of one of the best friends I ever had, a man who in matters of faith had the beautiful simplicity of a child and who endeavored to have the Sermon on the Mount wrought out in his daily life. Dr. Nathanael Burwash, the chancellor of Victoria College, further eulogized Eaton, saying that the old-fashioned fear of God and faith in Divine Providence was deep-rooted within him."[144]

"In 1909, Eaton's wife learned that the Methodists were trying to raise money to build the first great Methodist church in the northern section

"Old-fashioned fear of God and faith in Divine Providence was deep-rooted within him."

of Toronto. She offered to donate all the money they needed to build one of the handsomest churches in the city and made only one request: that they church be named after her husband. The Timothy Eaton Memorial Church, on Toronto's St. Clair Avenue, was completed in 1914. It testifies to Eaton's steadfast faith."[145]

ROBERT STANLEY WEIR (1856-1926)
Judge
Author of English Words to O Canada

"What sort of a man was Robert Stanley Weir?...A Canadian patriot, obviously. But his patriotism was not an aggressive nationalist boasting. It was something far more subtle...He was a man of much tenderness, as his voluntary visits to the crippled children reveal. And he was tender in his feeling for his country. The feeling in his lines O Canada (the same tender feeling for the land) appeared in one of the poems he wrote during the First World War. He pictured the Canadian soldier in the trench, under the pitiless rain. With shells screeching overhead, he still sees in memory his own faraway land:

"He was a man of much tenderness... and he was tender in his feeling for his country."

Smoke red the sun behind him falls — to rise
High into far-off, blue Canadian skies.
Above his head the shells are screaming —
But. Of the tender North he's dreaming.
Roar of the shattering guns and rain, rain, rain!
Will sun and silence never come again?
When, lo, behold the golden meadows,
The bending grain and soft cloud shadows!
The hearts of home, dear hearts and true,
Come dancing to him as they used to do,
With shouts of youth — its songs and laughter —
Though sighs, like echoes, follow after;
And summer days by peaceful wood and stream,
And tranced nights that throbbed with love and dream —
These, as the cold rain, pitiless drenches
Come to him, standing in the trenches."[146]

"Of [Weir] it can be truly said he was just in the exercise of power, generous in the protection of weakness, and beloved for his rare charm of kind courtesy to the timid souls of all classes...When such a man wrote the English version of O Canada his patriotism was not a vain boast; it was a profound sentiment, a thing of memory and the heart. As he believed all deep sentiments become religious, he felt the religious reality in the love of one's own land."[147]

"When such a man wrote the English version of O Canada his patriotism was not a vain boast; it was a profound sentiment, a thing of memory and the heart. As he believed all deep sentiments become religious, he felt the religious reality in the love of one's own land."

"The sprit of religious dedication in his poem was obscured and largely lost when the official adaptation of what he had written deleted the final verse. This lost verse reveals the religious context of the original version of O Canada:

Ruler Supreme,
Who hearest humble prayer,
Hold our Dominion
In Thy loving care.
Help us to find, O God, in Thee,
A lasting rich reward,
As waiting for a Better Day
We ever stand on guard.
Canada, glorious and free!
We stand on guard for Thee!"[148]

NELLIE MCCLUNG (1873-1951)

Renowned Author

Political and Social Activist

"Political activism in the service of social transformation and religious commitment were thus entwined for McClung from the beginning."

Nellie's mother in law, Annie McClung, "was instrumental in starting Nellie's writing career. Insisting that McClung enter a short story contest, Annie cared for the children and household while Nellie wrote. The story did not win the contest but it did become the opening chapter of McClung's first novel, *Sowing Seeds in Danny,* the Canadian best seller of 1908 and best-selling Canadian novel to that date."[149]

"Political activism in the service of social transformation and religious commitment were thus entwined for McClung from the beginning. Indeed her social gospel novel about the suffrage battle in Manitoba, *Purple Springs,* underscores her understanding that social activism was mandated by God."[150]

> **"McClung used her literature as a pulpit to preach her gospel."**

"Denied ordination by virtue of her sex, McClung used her literature as a pulpit to preach her gospel of feminist activism and social transformation."[151]

"Her fame as a novelist and skill as a public orator made her a potent political force when the battle to grant women the vote escalated. By 1914, McClung was giving speeches around the country in support of suffrage and temperance, to the dismay of her political opponents. Her efforts were catalytic; the right person at the right time."[152]

"McClung also actively lobbied for the ordination of women in the United Church of Canada, believing that 'Christ was a true democrat. He made no discrimination between men and women. They were all human beings to Him, with souls to save and lives to live, and He applied to men and women the same rule of conduct."[153]

> **"Nellie McClung's life reflects a passion for a cooperative community of equals, a vision grounded in the belief that God wishes our 'loving service, freely given.' "**

"Nellie McClung's life reflects a passion for a cooperative community of equals, a vision grounded in the belief that God wishes our 'loving service, freely given.' In *My Religion*, she lays this out clearly: 'It is not, "Chant my praises"; "Defend my theories"; "Kill my enemies." No, no — but a greater, better, lovelier task: "Feed my lambs." ' McClung was a best selling author, a political and social activist, and a forthright Christian whose liberal theology was grounded in a confidence that 'no one has a corner on light or grace.' She believed that faith should be professed in action and made her own life an example, struggling to overcome the prejudices of her culture in herself and in others."[154]

146

KING GEORGE VI (1895-1952)

"To those of my listeners who are young...
every one of you can be a pioneer, blazing by thought
and service a trail to better things.
Hold fast to all that is just and ofgood...
but strive also to improve and equalize that heritage
for all men and women in years to come.
Remember too that the key to all true progress
in life lies in faith, hope, and love.
May God give you their support."

1939 Address to Canada

"...There is one example in particular that North America can offer to other parts of the world...English and French have shown in Canada that they can keep their pride and distinctive culture...while yet combining to establish a broader freedom and security than either could have achieved alone...I would end with a special word of greeting to those of my listeners who are young...every one of you can be a pioneer, blazing by thought and service a trail to better things. Hold fast to all that is just and of good report in the heritage which your fathers have left to you, but strive also to improve and equalize that heritage for all men and women in years to come. Remember too that the key to all true progress in life lies in faith, hope, and love. May God give you their support, and may God help them to prevail."[155]

"Hold fast to all that is just and of good report in the heritage which your fathers have left you, but strive also to improve and equalize that heritage for all men and women in years to come."

148

AGNES MACPHAIL (1890-1954)

Politician

Canada's First Female Member of Parliament

"Faith played a meaningful role in her life."

"She emerged as one of the best orators in the House of Commons, but often found herself praying silently for guidance about how to vote."

"Following the 1921 Federal election, Agnes Macphail became the country's best-known woman as Canada's first female Member of Parliament. But Agnes was not celebrated primarily as a fighter for women's suffrage; her campaigns were mainly for cooperation and against war, for a better deal for the farmers, and against the existing Canadian penal system. In fact, though she fought to better the conditions of women, she walked into politics as if sexual differences did not exist. She fought as an equal with men for the issues that moved her."[156]

"While helping to organize local groups, Agnes gained recognition as a forceful speaker, leading to her 1921 federal candidacy on the

Farmer-Labour ticket and to her becoming the first woman member of the House of Commons."[157]

"She emerged as one of the best orators in the House of Commons, but often found herself praying silently for guidance about how to vote. Agnes supported the Progressives' anti-imperialism and their quest for Canadian autonomy, but it was her championing of the advancement of women, peace, and prison reform that really set her apart."[158]

"In 1929, her activity in the Women's International League for Peace and Freedom along with Lucy Woodsworth led to her being appointed as Canada's first woman delegate to the League of Nations in Geneva."[159]

"As prison populations burgeoned, Agnes intensified her efforts to end the inhumane treatment of criminals and the inordinately high recidivism rates that made beggars of inmates' wives and children."[160]

"…[F]aith played a meaningful role in her life. 'No one person built the church,' she reflected, 'but each had its part in something which by its very age and continuity became something more than the sum of them all.' She believed that to 'be happy we all need to lose our little spirits in the Great Spirit which is called God."[161]

"At her funeral, her minister eulogized: 'Her life might have been much easier. But this was the path she chose the craggy course.' "[162]

GEORGE P. VANIER (1888-1967)
Governor General from 1959-1967

"Let us first seek faith, faith in God above everything, faith in Christ and in his Church; and loyalty to our religious, moral and cultural heritage."

"Mr. Prime Minister, my first words are a prayer. May Almighty God in His infinite wisdom and mercy bless the sacred mission which has been entrusted to me by Her majesty the Queen and help me to fulfil in all humility. In exchange for His strength, I offer Him my weakness. May He give peace to this beloved land of ours, and to those who live in it, the grace of mutual understanding, respect and love...Let us give all our strength to this quest for unity, generosity, faith and loyalty. Let us first seek faith, faith in God above everything, faith in Christ and in his Church; and loyalty to our religious, moral and cultural heritage. Let us put our faith not so much to the traditions of our past as to their spirit, for only thus can our faith be open to the inspiration of the present and directed to the promise of the future."[163]

"Mr. Prime Minister, my first words are a prayer."

151

PAULINE VANIER (1898-1991)

"Pauline's early studies in Montréal's Sacred Heart Convent gave her a strong religious foundation, and her subsequent readings with a worldly-wise tutor of English and French literature developed her lively mind and insatiable curiosity. She early contemplated becoming a nun, but when the First World War broke out she immediately applied to join the army, as a foot soldier. Unsuccessful, she secretly enrolled in a nursing course and to her parent's dismay accepted a job at a military convalescent hospital, where she laboured long hours until the war's end."[164]

"The realm of justice and gentleness should prevail."

"When [her husband] George was named governor-general in 1959, Pauline...would become one of the most memorable First Ladies this country has ever known. She jumped into her new role with energy and fervour as the vice-regal couple crisscrossed the land visiting hospitals and schools, factories and prisons...Of all the causes she espoused, none was more important to her than the welfare of the family."[165]

She "served as the chancellor of the University of Ottawa, in whose affairs she showed a keen interest. At her investiture, she shared her idealistic and ecumenical hopes for the university's future. The realm of justice and gentleness should prevail, she said...Faith, far from being outmoded or old-fashioned, imparts a beauty, a richness, and a radiance that can be found in no other source."[166]

At the age of 73 she decided "she would move to France to join her son Jean, who had founded l'Arche, a community north of Paris for mentally handicapped adults."[167]

"Pauline Vanier invested her entire life with love, humour, service, compassion, and spiritual questing."[168]

> *"Faith, far from being outmoded or old-fashioned, imparts a beauty, a richness, and a radiance that can be found in no other source."*

JOHN DIEFENBAKER (1895-1979) AND PIERRE ELLIOT TRUDEAU (1919-2000)
Introduction of the Canadian Bill of Rights

> *"It begins with the Parliament of Canada affirming that the Canadian Nation is founded upon principles that acknowledge the supremacy of God."*

"In 1960, Prime Minister John Diefenbaker introduced the Canadian Bill of Rights. It begins with the Parliament of Canada affirming that the Canadian Nation is founded upon principles that acknowledge the supremacy of God...In 1981, Pierre Elliot Trudeau signed his name to the Canadian Charter of Rights and Freedoms. The Charter begins with, Whereas Canada is founded upon

153

principles that recognize the supremacy of God and the rule of the law."[169]

"Former PM, Pierre Trudeau, acknowledged the impact of Canada's Christian foundations by stating, 'The golden thread of faith is woven throughout the history of Canada, from its beginning up to the present time. Faith was more important than commerce in the minds of the many European explorers and settlers. Canadians owe a debt to the faith of our fathers and to the spiritual heritage which finds expression in countless ways in our daily lives.' "[170]

"Canadians owe a debt to the faith of our fathers and to the spiritual heritage which finds expression in countless ways in our daily lives."

SPEECH FROM THE THRONE
3rd Session, 37th Parliament of Canada.

"...[A]s you carry out your duties and exercise your responsibilities, may you be guided by Divine Providence."[171]

ERNEST MANNING (1908-1996)
Canada's Longest Standing Premier
Radio Show Host
Senator

"He spoke often of the need for national and spiritual revival and urged Christians to live in light of Jesus' imminent return."

"Ernest Manning is best remembered as Alberta's premier from 1943 to 1968 — the longest serving Premier in the Commonwealth — and as the host of *Canada's National Bible Hour* for nearly half a century. These dual roles exemplify his practice of integrating Christianity with every area of his life. He was prudent and careful in politics, always practicing Christian-based reconciliation and conflict resolution. Many Albertans were aware that his first call had been to the Christian ministry. Politics was a diversion. But Manning always held the view that both God and the people had some say in how long he would be premier — and he was not about to argue with either."[172]

Manning helped William "Bible Bill" Aberhart "found the Social Credit party, which won the 1935 Alberta election. Manning succeeded to the premiership on Aberhart's death in 1943."[173]

"Mannings premiership signaled the beginning of policies to pay down the province's debt and restore its fiscal credibility...Manning presided over a corruption-free government known for its populism

155

and its fiscal conservatism. His careful stewardship of the province's oil reserves and revenues and his skill in working with the oil industry's corporate leaders built his reputation for integrity."[174]

"Manning's understanding of the Scriptures gave him an appreciation of the human need as enunciated by proponents of the social gospel...he encouraged strong individual, corporate, and religious initiatives in addressing social issues."[175]

> *"His understanding of the Scriptures gave him an appreciation of the human need."*

"On his radio broadcasts, Manning emphasized the individual side of faith....His emphasis was on the life-changing effect of a commitment to Jesus Christ. And he wanted his listeners to understand that their parents, church, or good works could not make them Christians. As individuals they were responsible for their own spiritual condition and destiny."[176]

> *"His emphasis was on the life-changing effect of a commitment to Jesus Christ."*

"He spoke often of the need for national and spiritual revival and urged Christians to live in light of Jesus' imminent return...At its peak, the *National Bible Hour* was estimated to have six hundred thousand listeners from across Canada each week."[177].

"Strength, commitment, and reason marked Ernest Manning's presence in Alberta. Whether in matters of faith, politics, business or family, he emphasized the values of hard work, high ethical standards, compassion, and reliance on the goodness and grace of God. His political foes admitted that — almost without peer — he epitomized honesty and integrity in government. Ernest Manning was always careful to communicate that he could not have done so without the work of God in his heart and life."[178]

TAGAK CURLEY (1944-Present)
Father of Nunavut

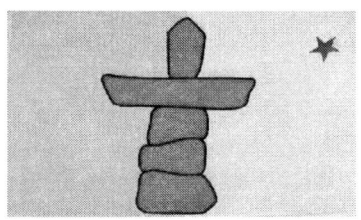

"He laid the spiritual foundations for a government rooted in the Word of God."

"Tagak Curley, founding president of the Inuit Brotherhood in 1971, commenced negotiations with the federal government in 1973 that led to the creation of Nunavut. He came to Christ during this process and laid the spiritual foundations for a government rooted in the Word of God. He was saved during one of the public services being held during the annual political meeting. God touched his life, healed his unforgiveness and gave him a love for all men everywhere. His prayer is that as Canadian families, it is most important that we continue to unite, not only for our own provinces, but that the hand of God be upon the whole nation of Canada. He is not alone. Women like Kay Gordon and men like John Spillenar have spent most of their adult lives being missionary pioneers to Canada's Inuit peoples. God's Word continues to inspire leaders to rebuild the broken altars of Canada's northland."[179]

"... [T]hat the hand of God be upon the whole nation of Canada."

CHAPTER 3:
•
IN CANADA'S NEWSPAPERS:

Confederation Day 1867
and Other Days

Following are excerpts from various Canadian newspapers on, or concerning, Confederation Day (1867). They reveal something of what was in the heart of Canadians all across the nation on the day that marks Canada's birth. They also give us a snap shot of the "well" of righteous dreams in our history and the Godly standards to which former generations in this country were committed. As I read these articles this thought crossed my mind: "Could it be that these words are an echo of God's heart for Canada?" I believe that they are and that the Spirit of God is searching all across our nation, and generation, looking for those who will willingly raise their voices for righteousness sake, in the public square, as these ones did.

Who will speak, write, and act in our day and in our generation? I pray that, as your read these quotes, you will not only be inspired but that something deep in your soul will be set ablaze with the LORD's "destiny dream" for Canada. I pray also that, as you read, a mantle for righteous revolution will fall upon you and that you will be compelled to boldly arise, when and where the Spirit of God leads you, to unashamedly proclaim His name and majesty in the public square of this nation.

The bold text in this chapter is added.

QUEBEC

MONTRÉAL DAILY
July 2nd, 1867
"The New Nation"
By H.K.C.

What more, Canadians, do we need?
The blessing of our God.
Let then, the warm petition rise,
Where village spires point to the skies,
Where city thousands meet for prayer
That Canada may ever be
Untied, happy, brace and free,
And honoured everywhere![180]

"What more
Canadians
do we need?
The blessing
of our God.
Let then warm
petitions rise."

MONTRÉAL DAILY WITNESS/
MONTRÉAL GAZETTE

July 1st, 1867
Dominion Day Poem
By John Read

I.

Our land is flushed with love; through the
    wealth of her gray-haired tresses,
From his bright-red fingers the sun has
    been dropping his armourous fire,
And her eyes are gladly oppressed with
    the weight of his lips caresses,
And the zephyr-throbs of her bosom keep
    time with the voice of his lyre.

*"The King
of the years
is crowning
our land
with His
glory of
love."*

II.

`Tis the noon of the sweet strong
    summer,the king of the months
    of the year,
And the king of the years is crowning
    our land with His glory of love,
And the king of all kings, in whose
    crown each gem is the light of
    the sphere,
Looks smilingly down on our land
    from the height of His heaven
    above.

*"And the king
of kings
...looks
smiling down
on our land*

III.

For to-day she breathes what to her is the first of a nation's
    breath,
As she lies neath the gaze of the sun, **as a bride**, or **a child**
    new-born,

Lies with fair motionless limbs in the beautiful semblance of
　　death,
Yet awake with the joy of a bird that awakens with the whisper of
　　morn.

IV.

And her soul is drinking the music that flows through the golden
　　lyre,
From the deeps of the woods and waters and wonderful hearts of
　　men,
From the long-hushed songs of the forest, the wild primeval
　　choir,
`**Till she feels the breath of the Spirit move over her face
　　again.**

V.

**So she hears, not in words but
　　in spirit, the changeful tale
　　of the past,**
As she leans to the sun with veins
　　that are blue like the blue
　　of sky,
**Hears with a smile on her lips
　　that the demon Division*
　　is cast into the river of
　　death, as a monster
　　worthy to die.**

*"So she hears, not in
words but in spirit,
the changeful tale
of past…that the
demon Division is
cast into the river of
death, as a monster
worthy to die."*

VI.

And she hears many tongues of men, that are singing as one in
　　her praise.
Calling her, all, by one name, a name that is noble and old.
Singing a poem of joy for the light of the gladdest of days.
**Making a noise of thanksgiving for a union more precious
　　than gold.**[181]

165

MONTRÉAL GAZETTE
July 1st, 1867
"Dominion Day"

Till now, **through God's good guiding**,
Those who as foremen strove,
With heart in heart confining,
As brothers join in love;
Till, from lake, sea and ocean,
Mountain and woody dell,
Is heard, with glad emotion.
Divisions* passing bell.[182]

"Is heard with
glad emotion,
Division's
passing bell."

*The division that the authors are speaking of in both this and the previous poem is that of the division between French and English speaking Canadians that had caused so much pain and devastation. Confederation was hoped by many to heal this division.

166

THE QUEBECER

July 4th, 1867

"To the Free and Independent Electors of the Country of Megantic"

By T. H. Grant

"Under Confederation we must rise to the dignity of a nation. The scenes of personal rancor, or sectional hate, and of party strife, that tarnish the annals of the past cannot be revived and if there must be difference of opinion, as undoubtedly there will be on all important questions, let them arise from an honest conviction of right, and from consciousness that the policy advocated is the one that will best promote the advancement of the country."[183]

"We must rise to the dignity of a nation. [The disunity] that tarnish the annals of the past cannot be revived."

THE MONTRÉAL DAILY

July 2nd, 1867

"Dominion Day"

"It would be difficult to imagine a more lovely day than the first of July 1867."

"The coldest heart that ever looked on heaven had surely felt the beauty of that day [Confederation Day]. It would be difficult to imagine a more lovely day than the first of July, 1867 — a day destined...to be a landmark in history."[184]

167

ONTARIO

THE TORONTO GLOBE & MAIL
July 1st, 1867
"Confederation Day, The Dominion
of Canada, Historical Notes"
By George Brown

We "fervently pray that all the blessings anticipated from the measure,
by its promoters, may be fully realized."[185]

OTTAWA CITIZEN
July 1st, 1867
"The New Dominion"
By Charles Sangster

Not in pride the firm foundations,
Of an Empire we lay;
Trusting in the God of Nations,
We would keep our Natal Day:
Trusting in that sacred promise,
Made to all those that believe
Will not now be wrested from us —
"Ask ye, and ye shall receive."

Ardent souls to-day are moving,
Heaven with prayers for this dear land;
Men whose hearts go forth in loving,
Every pebble on its strand.

"Not in pride the
firm foundations
of an empire we
lay; trusting in the
God of nations
we would keep our
Natal Day."

From New Brunswick's sea-washed
    harbours,
Rolls the prayerful wavelet on;
Through the wilds and sunny arbors
Of the far Saskatchewan.

Hear us then, mysterious Power,
God, whom all the earth shall own,
Make this an auspicious hour,
Lay for us our cornerstone;
Lift Thy hands in blessings o'er us,
Bless us, Lord, from sea to sea,
Pointing to the hopes before us,
And the future yet to be.

"Hear us then, mysterious Power, God, whom all the earth shall own. Make this an auspicious hour, lay for us our cornerstone."

Could we leave the past behind us,
Party rancor, priestly strife
So that every day would find us,
Rising to the higher life;
Could we with stern endeavor
Hand in hand begin the race,
Then among the nations ever
We might hold our lawful place.

Brothers, from whatever far land,
From what chime beneath the sun,
Here, to-day, in this our Norland,
Duty cries we *must* be one;
One with hopes that may not falter,
One with hearts as true as steel,
That no time nor change can alter
Through all coming woe or weal...

"Could we leave the past behind us, party rancor, priestly strife...Then among the nations ever we might hold our lawful place."

Land to which my hopes are clinging,
Proudly as our rivers swell
Is the voice of Freedom ringing
Round the hopes we love so well:
Keep that noble spirit centred
Firmly in each loving heart;
From the souls where once it entered
Let it never more depart.

But with Truth and Justice banding,
Throned within our council halls,
With its godlike form commanding
Like an angel on the walls;
Terror to the evil-doer,
Friend to Right and foe to Wrong,
But a sweet and gentle wooer
Where the heart is lean and strong.

Holy Love fill all our bowers,
Gentle Peace imbue the sod;
All the future may be ours,
But today belongs to God!
He hath laid our broad foundations,
Leaving us to build thereon;
Lo, we stand among the Nations,
God our living cornerstone![186]

"Holy Love fill all
our bowers, gentle
peace imbue the
sod; All the future
may be ours, but
today belongs to
God! He hath
laid our broad
foundations,
Leaving us to
build thereon, Lo,
we stand among
the Nations,
God our living
cornerstone!"

THE DAILY GLOBE (TORONTO)
"Canada —
A Confederation Ode"
By Edward Hartley Dewart

God bless our noble Canada,
God bless the new Dominion
Where law and liberty have sway,
No one of all her sons today
Is tyrant's serf or minion.

*"God bless our
noble Canada,
God bless the new
Dominion."*

Give joy a tongue, let peaceful mirth
Dispel all faithless fears —
We hail a youthful nation's birth,
Who in the wondering eyes of Earth
Takes rank among her peers.

Fling out our banner to the breeze.
And proudly greet the world
With words of smity and peace,
For never on more halcyon seas
Was Freedom's flag unfurled.

Thrice hail our own beloved land
By God to freeman given:
We seek no distant golden strand, —
Nor other time shall we demand,
Till home we find in Heaven.

*"By God to
freeman given. We
seek no distant
golden strand...Till
home we find
in heaven."*

We boast no charms of high degree
In wealth in rank, or blood,
No tales of mighty chivalry —
Long lines or lordy ancestry —
Nor haunted stream or wood.

Few proud historic names have we,
Whose memory thrills the heart —
No scenes of embalmed Poise —
No hoary castles grand to see —
The pride of ancient art.

But though the Past may barren be,
In battle, long, and story,
The future is fair to view,
Gleaming with morning's youthful dew,
And bright with coming glory.

I love thee noble Canada,
Thou cradle of the free
Where're my coming feet may stray —
Whatever site may come — I pray
That God may shelter thee

I love thy forests grand; there too
In youth loved to rove —
Thy trees, thy flowers of valued blue —
I love thy glorious lakes, as blue
As vast as heaven above.

I love thy green and towering hills —
Thy valleys rich and fair,
Where wealth in pearly dew distills —
Thy cool maundering forest rills,
Hid from the summer glare.

I love thy rivers broad and free —
Thy cataracts sublime,
Where God unveils his majesty —
Whose hymns make grandest melody,
That strikes the ear of Time.

"I love thee noble Canada... Whatever site may come – I pray that God may shelter thee."

"I love thy rivers broad and free – thy cataracts sublime, where God unveils his majesty."

172

I love thy bright and balmy spring —
Thy leafy summer bowers,
Where gay thy woodland songster sing,
And every zephyrm its wing
Bears scent of fragrant flowers.

I love when Autumn's brilliant dyes
Thy forest foliage stain,
And Nature yields her rich supplies —
When Winder ermine mantle lies
On river, hill and plain.

I love thy homes whose light retains,
Brave sons and daughters fair,
Where liberty with truth remains,
And every loyal heart disdains
A servile yoke to wear.[187]

NEW BRUNSWICK

SAINT JOHN
NEW BRUNSWICK MORNING NEWS
July 3rd, 1867
"New Dominion Holiday"

"The more loyal, patriotic and, overwhelmingly more numerous portion of the lieges pronounce [Confederation] a marriage, and in this they also are correct. It was the consummation of a Union, which both reason, experience and history, warrant us in asserting will ultimately prove conducive to the happiness and interest of all concerned. Mankind generally lean rather favourably towards matrimony, and as a rule wish to honour it."[188]

"It was the consummation of a Union."

"[On the morning of Confederation Day bells] awakened both the echoes and the slumbering citizens of all the surrounding districts by a salute of twenty-one guns, fired in honour of this greatest of all modern marriages."[189]

"Greatest of all modern marriages."

THE NEW BRUNSWICK REPORTER

June 28th, 1867

"The work of consummating the Union goes bravely on."

"...The work of consummating the Union goes bravely on."[190]

"...The deliberations of the Privy Council have been conducted in the most harmonious spirit, boding well for future unanimity and power."[191]

THE NEW BRUNSWICK MORNING NEWS

July 1st, 1867

"We cherish high expectations of our future prosperity for the New Dominion...The resources of the Dominion are varied and great; and the spirit of its people will rise to a level with their position and their opportunities. The Dominion will make for itself a name in the world worthy of the honoured stock from which its people sprang. Its sons, always proud of their ancestry, will soon grow proud of their country."[192]

THE NEW BRUNSWICK REPORTER

July 5th, 1867

"The New Dominion"

> *"From Halifax to Sarnia we are one people."*

"From Halifax to Sarnia we are one people…we can now take our place among the States of the earth, proud of our inheritance."[193]

"…[I]t is not the time now to recount the struggles and strife which gave it birth; but rather…by a blending of common interests, and united effort give it a sure foundation and a permanent existence."[194]

"…[W]e can look forward to a good time coming."[195]

SAINT JOHN NEW BRUNSWICK MORNING NEWS

July 3rd 1867

"Organization Complete"

By Edward Willis

"We wish the ministry success, and we trust that its members, one and all, will prove by their acts that they are worthy of the occasion which has called them forth, as well as fitting guardians of the sacred trust placed for the present in their keeping."[196]

"…[F]rom the windows of stores and private residences, and from the lofty masts of the shipping in the harbor, the flag of our nation, at once, the emblem of liberty and the symbol of freedom, floated gaily in the breeze."[197]

SAINT JOHN NEW BRUNSWICK
MORNING NEWS

July 1st, 1867
"The Nation's Birthday"
By Melville

Let our voices be heard on this glorious morn
In anthems of joy, a NATION is born;
A companion for her who rules o'er the wave —
The foe of the tyrant — the friend of the slave.

Born — not `mid the battle-field's carnage and woe,
Where father and brother and friend are laid low;
Born away on the breast of the crimson dye wave
From the glory of life to the gloom of the grave.

Her form rises not from the ashes of death,
Her brow is untouched by war's pestilent breath;
Crime breathes not the air which refreshes her life,
And ne'er has she gazed on the red
> **flag of strife.**

But the sword which has slain every
> **foe in her way,**
Severs not the clear ties of fond
> **hearts in its play;**
It leaves not a dark stain of horror
> **behind —**
'Tis the bright sword of TRUTH —
> **the weapon of MIND.**

> *"Ne'er has she gazed on the red flag of strife...The sword which has slain every foe in her way...'Tis the bright sword of TRUTH."*

It flashed in the sunlight of earth's
dawning hour,
And gleamed `mid the darkness of tyranny's power...

And ne'er has it conquered error's dark night,
Or swift put the foes of progression to flight,
Which such effortless power as it conquers today,
And CANADA draws her first breath 'neath its sway.

Yes, our Nation is born on the bosom of Peace;
May her glory grow bright and her power increase;
O'er her head may no cloud of adversity rise,
But smooth be her pathway and stormless her skies.

And may God whom the
       Heavens doth hide.
Be our country's defender,
       her guardian and guide;
That CANADA ne'er from
       her seat may be hurled,
`Till she falls in her might
       with the fall of the
World.[198]

"And may God whom the Heavens doth hide. Be our country's defender, her guardian and guide."

NEWFOUNDLAND

THE NEWFOUNDLANDER NEWSPAPER
July 2nd, 1867

"This Union gives promise of a prosperity and greatness that will attract the wonder of older nations."

"Yesterday was the birth-day of the new Confederation. We have no doubt we shall hear in due time that its inauguration was worthily celebrated by those whose nationality has dawned under such bright auspices and who cannot but be filled with high hopes for their future career. Whether viewed commercially, politically or socially this Union gives promise of a prosperity and greatness which will attract the wonder of older nations and the many powerful and resolute agencies enlisted to accomplish this result ought to silence all doubt as to its speedy realization."[199]

"For the evils arising from conditions to so great an extent antagonistic, and of capabilities so largely wasted, they have now found the aptest remedy."[200]

"We may well forcast a brilliant future."

"For a Confederacy so organized and invigorated we may well forecast a brilliant future, and this future in abundant measure we cordially wish to the new Dominion, with a desire no less ardent that ere long Newfoundland may take its rightful place as a member of the Union."[201]

"Services [to pray for the new Dominion] were held...[At a]bout 10 o'clock the Rev. Dr. Richey took the stand on the Parade, and delivered the 'oration' of the day...he expects greater benefits to follow Confederation."[202]

THE COURIER

July 3rd, 1867
"North American Confederation"

The Dominion of Canada "is rich in every element."[203]

NOVA SCOTIA

THE BRITISH COLONIST
June 29th, 1867
"The Birth of the New Dominion"

All Hail to the day!
Bright and glorious day!
A joyous one let it be,
That joins us forever,
    in bonds none can sever,
Uniting the loyal and free.

"All Hail to the day!
...That joins us
forever, in bonds
none can sever."

A Day big with fate — a young nation's hope,
Is sealed by a happy alliance.
A union of strength, protection, defence,
Bids the foes of our country defiance.

A day that will long be remembered by all,
As the dawn of our National birth,
When on this side the world, our Flag we unfurled,
Over our new "Dominion on Earth."

A Dominion whose prospects are
    charming and bright,
Whose pathway looks sunny and clear,
With God as our friend,
    our rights to defend,
We have naught
    in the future to fear...[204]

"With God as
our friend, our
rights to defend,
we have naught
in the future
to fear."

180

HALIFAX COLONIST

July 2nd, 1867

"Tuesday Morning, July 2"

"We are a united people...we have everything to inspire us with hope and confidence."

"Yesterday we entered on the new epoch of our history...The days of isolation and dwarf-hood are past...we are a united people...we have every thing to inspire us with hope and confidence...no perennial grievances demanding redress, no long-standing sore threatening to destroy the fabric of our political system. No cry for rights withheld or liberties denied can disturb the peace of our society."[205]

ACADIAN RECORDER

July 6th, 1867

"What God Hath Joined"[22]

By Phoebe Cary

"Love is as strong as death...Many waters cannot quench love, neither can the floods drown it." Song of Songs 8:6

That the cords of love must be strong as death,
If they hold and keep a heart;
Not daisy chains, that snap in the breeze,
Or break with their weight apart!

---

[22] This poem does not overtly refer to Confederation though there is a chance it relates to it. It has been included in the research both because it was published in the Acadian Recorder on Confederation week and because it is directly in line with the theme of "Holy Matrimony" that is used to describe Confederation in other news publications this same week.

For the pretty colors of youth's sweet morn
Fade out from the noonday sky,
And blushing love in the rose born,
Alas! With the roses die!

But the faith that when our morn is past
Tender and true survives,
Is the faith we need to lean upon
In the crisis of our lives: —
The love that: shines in the eye grown dim,
In the voice that trembles speaks,
And sees the roses that years ago
Withered and died in our cheeks.

That sheds its halo round us still
Of soft immortal light,
When we change youth's golden coronal
For a crown of silver white.
A love for sickness, and for health,
For rapture and for tears;
That will live for us, and bear with us,
Through all our mortal years.

And such there is: — there are lovers here,
On the brink of the grave that stand,
Who shall cross to the hill beyond,
and walk forever hand in hand.
Pray youth and maid, that your mate be theirs
Who are joined no more to part,
For death comes not to the loving soul,
Nor age to the loving heart.[206]

HALIFAX EVENING REPORTER
June 29th, 1867
"National Day"

"...[W]e have the Union of the Colonies a fixed fact....When before has such an event been seen?...On Monday...'LONG LIVE THE NEW DOMINION,' will be shouted over the land and Canada [is] a union obtained with no cost of blood."[207]

"Over the whole land many a prayer will ascend to the Almighty Disposer of human affairs that this union now accomplished may be a blessed one — one fruitful of happiness to the living generation, and to the future one who shall take the place of the present...the heart — uttered prayers, are all indications that the national principle is as operative upon us as upon any other people."[208]

"Over the whole land many a prayer will ascend to the Almighty Disposer of human affairs that this union now accomplished may be a blessed one."

"The secret of greatness and prosperity lies in our rising above...-sectional feelings...and ascending to that national, patriotic spirit which ought to animate us."[209]

"Past opposition will be buried."

"The Dominion is for us, why should we not all be for the Dominion?...enmities, past opposition will be buried...when the annual return of the day recalls the memory of the first day of the Dominion, fathers...will tell to their children."[210]

THE HALIFAX REPORTER

July 2nd, 1867

"The Great Union Demonstration — Grand Triumph of British Sentiment — Union Proclaimed"

By Joseph C. Crosskill

"Yesterday will long be remembered by our citizens. Many now boys and girls will delight to tell by the fireside, when their heads are crowned with silvered locks, how they were present at the celebration of the first day of the new era that has burst upon us."[211]

HALIFAX CITIZEN

July 13th, 1867

"…[O]ur new dominion is to be a very great country."[212]

IN THE NEWS
ON OTHER DAYS

THE OTTAWA CITIZEN
FIRST DAY OF PARLIAMENT
November 8th, 1867
Speech from the Throne
Governor General Lord Monk

"I am happy to be able to congratulate you on the abundant harvest with which it has pleased Providence to bless the country, and on the general prosperity of the Dominion. Your new nationality enters on its coats backed by the moral support — the material aid — and the most ardent good wishes of the Mother Country. Within your own borders peace security and propriety prevail, and I fervently pray that your aspirations may be directed to such high and patriotic objects, and that you may be inspired with such a spirit of moderation and wisdom as will cause you to tender the great work of the Union, which has achieved blessing for yourselves and your posterity, and a fresh starting point in the moral, political and material advancement of the people of Canada."[213]

"I am happy to be able to congratulate you on the abundant harvest with which it has pleased Providence to bless this country."

NEWS OF FRUITFULNESS ON THE LAND SURROUNDING CONFEDERATION

While searching through the newspaper archives for clues as to what was in the heart of the nation on the first day of Confederation I was amazed to find these two articles. They reported of how both the harvest and the fish yield had been poor in the years prior to Confederation. However, on the first day of the new nation a good report came: both the harvest and the fish yield were looking strong! Scripture is clear that when the inhabitants of the land are walking in righteousness and honouring God that this health in the spirit will be reflected in a healthy land physically.[23] . These clippings are so encouraging because they give evidence that something was right about Confederation Day 1867! I believe this good report could be direct evidence of the Lord's pleasure over the new union called the Dominion of Canada.

---

[23] For excellent teaching on how righteousness affects the physical land and agriculture I encourage you to read Alistair Petrie's book, **Releasing Heaven on Earth,** or go to resources by Gwen Shaw of End-Time Handmaidens and Servants.

HALIFAX MORNING CHRONICLE
July 1st, 1867: Good Fish Yield
"Newfoundland"

"Providence promises the answer...most bountifully this season...We have just concluded a good seal fishery — one better than we have been recently accustomed to...Many planters west of the capital have more fish caught now than they took in all last year, and others to the north are doing as well...The success already realized...gives life and hope to our fishermen."[214]

THE QUEBEC DAILY NEWS
July 4th, 1867: Good Harvest
"The Harvest"

"Throughout the length and breadth of the country we hear the most favourable accounts of the prospects of the crop. It is to be hoped that a kind Providence will not disappoint the expectations which are indulged in relation to the harvests."[215]

CHAPTER 4:
•
CANADA'S SONG:

Current National Anthem
&
Other Lyrical
Submissions

The national anthem of any country is a telling picture of the values, hopes and dreams that lie in the heart of that nation. This section presents current lyrics of the Canadian national anthem from both the French and English versions. Following these are examples of other lyrics that were both used and submitted for consideration throughout our history.

Read, be encouraged and let us fight for these righteous dreams (many of which, I believe, reflect the LORD's dreams for Canada) to come to pass!

Let us pray in accordance with our anthem:

Ruler Supreme,
Who hearest humble prayer,
Hold our Dominion in Thy loving care,
Help us to find, O God, in Thee,
A lasting, rich reward,
As waiting for the better day
We ever stand on guard.[216]

The bold text in this chapter is added.

O Canada

Calixa Lavallée 1880

CURRENT FRENCH VERSION

BY JUDGE A. B. ROUTHIER

O Canada! Land of our forefathers
Your brow is crowned
with glorious jewels.
For your arm knows
how to carry the sword,
It knows how to carry the cross;
Your history is an epic
Of the most brilliant exploits;
And your valor, tempered with faith,
Will protect our homes and rights.
Under the eye of God,
Near the giant river,
The Canadian grows up in hope,
He is born of a proud race;
His childhood was blessed.
Heaven stamped his life in this new world;
Guided always by its light,
He will defend the honor of his flag.
Like his patron saint,[24]
 herald of the true God,
He bears on his brow the halo of fire.
Enemy of tyranny,
But friend of loyalty,
He knows how to defend in harmony
His proud liberty,
And by the force of his spirit thy
         immortal

*"For your arm
knows how to
carry the sword,
it knows how to
carry the cross."*

*"Sacred love of the
throne and altar,
fill our hearts
with your
immortal
inspiration."*

---

[24] See pages 81-84 regarding Canada's patron saint, Jean Brébeuf.

To establish the truth of our soil.
Sacred love of the throne and altar,
Fill our hearts with your immortal inspiration.

Among alien races
Our guide is the law;
May we know how to be a people of brothers
Under the yoke of the Faith;
And let us repeat, as our fathers did,
The conqueror's cry: **For Christ** and the King![217]

FORMER VERSIONS BY JUDGE A. B. ROUTHIER

O Canada, Our Fathers' land of old,
Thy brow is crown'd with leaves of
red and gold.
Beneath the shade of the Holy Cross,
Thy children own their birth.
No stains thy annals gloss,
Since valor shields thy hearth.
Almighty God! On Thee we call,
Defend our rights, forefend this nations thrall.
Altar and throne
Command our sacred love,
And mankind to us shall ever brothers prove.
Kings of Kings with Thy mighty breath,
All our sons do Thou inspire.

"Thy brow is crown'd with leaves of red and gold beneath the shade of the Holy Cross."

May no craven terror of life or death,
E'er damp the patriot's fire
Our might call
Loudly shall ring,
As in the days of old,
"For **Christ** and the King!"
As in the days of old,
"For **Christ** and the King!"

"King of Kings
with Thy
mighty breath
all our sons
do Thou inspire."

O Canada! Our fair ancestral land!
Crowning thy brow soft glows a starry band.
Thy loyal arm the sword can wield,
The cross it bears on high
Thy loyal arm the sword can wield,
The cross it bears on high,
The cross deeds of valor are a shield
To guard and glorify.
By faith imbued with guiding lights,
Thy valor guards our hearths and all our rights,
Thy valor guards our hearths and all our rights,
O sacred love of altar and of throne,
Fill all our hearts with Thy immortal tone.
With foreign nations peace prevail.
And law and justice guide.
As brothers, all our people hail abide.
And comradeship abide.
Canada! Repeat and sing.
Our fathers' victory call:
"For **Christ** and King!"
Our fathers' victory:
"For **Christ** and King!"[218]

CURRENT ENGLISH VERSION
BY ROBERT STANLEY WEIR

O Canada! Our home and native land!
True patriot love in all thy sons command;
With glowing hearts we see thee rise,
The true North, strong and free
From far and wide, O Canada
We stand on guard, for thee.
God keep our land,
Glorious and free,
O Canada, we stand guard for thee.
O Canada! Where pines and maples grow,
Great prairies spread and lordly rivers flow,
How dear to us thy broad domain,
From East to Western sea,
Thou land of hope for all who toil!
Thou true North, strong and free!
Canada! Beneath thy shining skies,
May stalwart sons and gentle maidens rise,
To keep thee steadfast through the years
From East to Western sea,
Our own beloved native land!
Our true North, strong and free!
Ruler Supreme,
       who hearest humble prayer,
Hold our Dominion
       in Thy loving care,
Help us to find, O God, in Thee,
A lasting, rich reward,
As waiting for the better day
We ever stand on guard.[219]

"God keep our land, glorious and free. O Canada, we stand on guard for thee."

"Ruler Supreme, who hearest humble prayer, Hold our Dominion in Thy loving care."

196

NATIONAL ANTHEM ACT

"By 1980, the Parliament, in the National Anthem Act, further added the phrase 'God keep our land glorious and free!' to our National Anthem to the poem written by Robert Stanley Weir back in 1908...Indeed, the National Anthem was a public prayer meant to be sung by the whole nation! Canada historically recognized the supremacy of God!"[220]

"The national anthem was a public prayer meant to be sung by the whole nation!"

OTHER LYRICAL SUBMISSIONS

FROM THE HYMNARY OF THE UNITED CHURCH OF CANADA (1930) BY ALBERT WATSON

Lord of the Lands, beneath Thy
    bending skies,
On field and flood, where're our
    banner flies,
Thy people lift their hearts to thee,
Their grateful hearts they raise:
May our Dominion ever be,
A temple of thy praise.
Thy will alone, let all enthrone;
Lord of the Lands, make Canada Thine own;
Lord of the Lands, make Canada Thine own!
Almighty Love, by Thy mysterious power,
In wisdom guide, with faith and freedom dower;
Be ours a nation ever more
That no oppression blights,
Where justice rules from shore to shore,
From lakes to northern lights.
May love alone for wrong atone;
Lord of the Lands, make Canada Thine own;
Lord of the Lands, make Canada Thine own!
Lord of the Worlds,
With strong eternal hand,
Hold us in honour,
Truth and self command;
The loyal heart, the constant mind,

"May our Dominion ever be a temple of thy praise. Thy will alone, let all enthrone."

"Lord of the Lands, make Canada Thine own."

The courage to be true,
Our wide extending Empire bind,
And all the earth renew.
Thy Name be known through every zone;
Lord of the Lands make Canada Thine own;
Lord of the Lands make Canada Thine own![225]

VERSION BY BISHOP C. VENN PILCHER

O Canada, our land, our love,
    our pride,
Bought by the blood of men who
    dared and died;
From East to West we loyal stand
By prairie lake and sea,
And pledge with joy both heart and hand
To God, to King, to thee!
Steadfast in mind stand we combined,
Mighty to serve our country,
    serve mankind!
Canada, our land, our pride, our love,
High be thine aim, all selfish aims above;
Thy maple leaves, blood-red recall
Christ's cross of splendid pain;
Thy golden sheaves, made bread for all,
His life, whose death was gain:
Thine be this mind!
God's prize to find,
Follow the Christ who calls thee,
calls mankind.[222]

"Bought by the blood of men who dared and died."

"Thy maple leaves, blood-red recall Christ's cross of splendid pain; Thy golden sheaves, made bread for all, His life, whose death was gain."

SUBMISSION BY MERCY E. POWELL MCCULLOCH

"In July 1908 Collier's Weekly an American magazine, established a Canadian edition under H. F. Gadsby. One of the editor's first acts was to institute a prize competition for an English text to Lavallee's tune. It was won by Mercy E. Powell McCulloch but her poem has not become widely know."[223]

"Lord God of Hosts! We now implore, bless our dear land this day and evermore.

Oh Canada!
In praise of thee we sing;
From echoing hills our anthems proudly ring.
With fertile plains, and mountains grand,
With lakes and rivers clear,
Eternal beauty, thou dost stand
Throughout the changing year.
Lord God of Hosts! We now implore,
Bless our dear land this day and evermore,
Bless our dear land this day and evermore.
Dear Canada! For thee our fathers wrought;
Thy good and ours unselfishly they sought.
With steadfast hand and fearless mind
They felled the forest domes,
Content at last to leave behind
A heritage of homes.
Lord God of Hosts!
Bless Canada! The homeland that we love;
Thy freedom came a gift from God above,
Thy righteous laws, thy justice fair,
We thank our God that we may share
Thy glorious destiny.
Lord God of Hosts.[224]

SUBMISSION BY
THE HON. JUDGE

Canada, beloved Country, thou!
**Hope's holy wreath adorning thy
young brow.**
Thine arm the sword has taken
To guard the faith of Christ;
Thy fealty unshaken
With valour keepeth tyst.
Lord of hosts; on Thee we call!
Protect our inland fields, our seaward wall.
Our annals glow with deeds of mighty men
Who conquered fate, undaunted, one to ten.
Alone, true hero-hearted
They kept our flag out-flung,
When all save honour parted
On glorious fields unsung.
O, Lord of hosts; may we recall
Their valourous deeds, and like
them stand or fall.
In this great West, where destiny awaits,
Two mighty oceans front her seaward gates.
May loyalty and honour,
Hold all her marts within,
Her skies that shine upon her,
Know all her myriads kin.
O, Lord of hosts; from these our coasts
Drive out all sordid greeds, all foolish boasts.
May love, revered of altar and throne,
Join these our hearts for truth so stand alone!
Our laws from their pure foundations
Their liberties prolong;
Till round our lakes and mountains
Fades out the world's old wrong.

*"Lord of hosts,
on Thee
we call!"*

*"Our annals
glow with deeds of
mighty men."*

O, Lord of hosts; to Thee we cling.
And shout our battle song,
"For Christ and the king!"[225]

*"Lord of hosts,
to Thee we cling."*

SUBMISSION BY
GEORGE CLARK HOLLAND

O Canada our own dear favoured land,
Dowered art thou by Nature's lavish hand.
All the wealth in thine of the streams and hills,
Of herds that roam the plain:
Thine the fruitful soil that the freeman tills
And treasure of the main.
Trusting in God, fearlessly hold
All thine inheritance from
             days of old
Dauntless their hearts, not counting
             gain or loss.
Who braved the wilds to win thee
             for the Cross,
On the hallowed field of the
             fateful Plain,
Was written Heaven's decree,
That through endless ages thy
             broad domain
Should Freedom's dwelling be
God be thy shield when conflicts rage,
Guarding inviolate thy heritage.
O Canada, our hopes are all in thee,
Firmly pursue thy glorious destiny.
With the flight of years may thy power expand,
Thy people's fame increase;
May the loyal children united stand
For brotherhood and peace.
Land beloved, God be thy guide,
Leading thee onward in an empire wide.[226]

*"Dauntless their
hears, not counting
gain or loss. Who
braved the wilds
to win thee
for the Cross."*

SUBMISSION BY HAROLD BOULTON

"First, Cross in hand."

Canada! The homeland we adore
God give us grace to love thee more and more!
From our Eastern sea to our Western sea
How wonderful in majesty
The realm thy sons control
We stand for thee, faithful and free
What e'er our birth, Canadians hear and soul
All hail to you brave gentlemen of France!
First, Cross in hand, you banners to advance;
To achieve that glorious goal.
And now we know one flag, one name,
And one harmonious whole,
One brother band linked hand in hand
What e'er our birth, Canadians heart and soul.
Giants of the west, our cloud-capped mountains stand,
Whose fruitful flanks toward sunlit seas expand;
Oh! The ripe what crowning the prairie farms
Is a glowing aureole,
Our forests vast reach out their arms
Where mighty waters roll;
We feel their call.
We love them all.
What o'er our birth,
Canadians heart and soul.
Canada! What must thy future hold,
When those to come thy scroll of fate unfold
Give a welcome warm to thy sons to be,
Who in these ranks enroll.
Where loyalty and liberty
Ten thousand miles patrol,
Strong may they be, faithful and free
"What e'er their birth, Canadians heart and soul."[227]

CHAPTER 5:
•
CANADA'S NAME
FLAG & CREST

CANADA'S NAME

A name says a lot. Throughout the word of God the importance of names is reiterated. Names often signify something regarding the conditions surrounding birth, the identity or the destiny of the one being born. As such, I felt it was important to do some "dusting" to find out where Canada's name actually comes from and what it means. I believe the meaning of our name gives a view into our call and destiny as a nation – a call and destiny that the LORD is looking for us to rise into with greater, Heaven blessed, glory. The section is short yet from it we can see a couple things clearly:

1. *The LORD has designed that Canada would be a dwelling place and a gathering place for the nations.*

2. *The LORD has purposed that He will have dominion from sea to sea. (This purpose is clearly reflected through the LORD's initiative to put it on the hearts of the Founding Fathers to set it into our very foundation and name.)*

How encouraging and powerful! Let us fight to see the fullness of this God ordained destiny come to pass!

In accordance with our name let us pray right now:

Father, we pray that our nation would indeed continue to be a settlement for the nations and that as You gather all the nations here that You would also gather them to Yourself. We pray that Canada would be a dwelling place for Your glory and Your glory alone; that You would have dominion from sea to sea and from the river to the ends of the earth, for Your name's sake! Amen!

"In 1535, two Indian youth told Jacques Cartier about the route to 'kanata.' They were referring to the village of Stadacona; 'kanata' was simply the Huron-Iroquois word for 'village' or 'settlement.' But for want of another name, Cartier used 'Canada' to refer not only to Stadacona (the site of present day Quebec City), but also to the entire area subject to its chief, Donnacona. The name was soon applied to a much larger area: maps in 1547 designated everything north of the St. Lawrence River as 'Canada.' Cartier also called the St. Lawrence River the 'Rivière de Canada', a name used until the early 1600s. By 1616, although the entire region was known as New France, the area along the great river of Canada and the Gulf of St. Lawrence was still called Canada. Soon explorers and fur traders opened up territory to the west and to the south and the area depicted as 'Canada' grew. In the early 1700s, the name referred to all lands in what is now the American Midwest and as far south as the present day Louisiana. The first use of 'Canada' as an official name came in 1791 when the Province of Quebec was divided into the colonies of Upper and Lower Canada. In 1841, the two Canadas were again united under one name, the Province of Canada. At the time of Confederation, the new country assumed the name of Canada."[228]

THE CHOOSING OF OUR NAME: "THE DOMINION OF CANADA"

(Reiteration from Chapter 2.)

"When the Fathers of Confederation were assembled discussing the terms and conditions of Confederation and the drafting of the British North America Act there had been considerable discussion the day before and many suggestions as to what the new United Canada should be called, and no conclusion had been reached. The discussion on the name stood over until the next day. The next morning, as was Sir Leonard's custom, he read a chapter from the Bible, and that particular morning he read Psalm Seventy-two. When reading verse eight of the Psalm, 'He shall have Dominion also from sea to sea,' the thought occurred to him, what a splendid name to give Canada. When he went back to the sitting of the convention that morning he suggested the word Dominion, which was agreed to, and Canada was called the Dominion of Canada. A letter signed by John A. Macdonald explained to Queen Victoria that the name was a tribute to the principles they earnestly desired to uphold."[229]

"A letter signed by John A. Macdonald explained to Queen Victoria that the name was a tribute to the principles they earnestly desired to uphold."

CANADA'S FLAG & CREST

Like its anthem, and name, the flag and crest of a nation can reveal something of a nation's DNA and call. This section is a brief chronology of our flag's evolution as well as some key remarks made regarding the flag. This section also includes information regarding the national crest. I pray you are encouraged and inspired as you see the many references to Christianity in the symbolism of both the Canadian crest and the various flags over the generations.

MAPLE LEAF

"The Canadian Red Ensign was replaced by the red and white maple leaf flag on February 15, 1965."[230]

LESTER B. PEARSON
Prime Minister
Canadian Flag Dedication Speech

"We salute the future, but we honour the past on which the future rests."

"...We salute the future, but we honour the past on which the future rests. As the symbol of a new chapter in our national story, our Maple Leaf Flag will become a symbol of that unity in our country without which one cannot grow in strength and purpose; the unity that encourages the equal partnership of two peoples on which this Confederation was founded; the unity also that recognizes the contributions and the cultures of many other races...May the land over which this new Flag flies remain united in freedom and justice; a land of decent

212

God-fearing people; fair and generous in all its dealings; sensitive, tolerant and compassionate towards all men; industrious, energetic, resolute; wise, and just in the giving of security and opportunity equally to all its cultures; and strong in its adherence to those moral principles which are the only sure guide to greatness. Under this Flag may our youth find new inspiration for loyalty to Canada; for a patriotism based not on any mean or narrow nationalism, but on the deep and equal pride that all Canadians will feel for every part of this good land. God bless our Flag! And God bless Canada!"[231]

"May the land over which this new Flag flies remain united in freedom and justice; a land of decent God fearing people... strong in its adherence to those moral principles which are the only sure guide to greatness.... God bless our flag! And God bless Canada! "

Remarks from David Mainse
(100 Huntley Street)
Regarding Canada's
Flag and Destiny

"...[W]e sang 'O Canada', and as we did, I found my eye drawn to that huge maple leaf on the flag overhead. 'You know', I said to the people when we had finished, 'ours is the only flag in the world with a leaf on it. And there's a verse in Scripture which talks about a tree of life, the leaves of which would be for the healing of the nations. I believe that this may well be Canada's role: to serve the rest of the world in prayer. When Billy Graham was on 100 Huntley Street a while back, he said that Canada may never be a military superpower, or an economic superpower, but she could become a spiritual superpower, showing the rest of the world the way. And when he said that, a number of us had the spine-tingling feeling that he was speaking prophetically.' "[232]

"And there's a verse in Scripture which talks about a tree of life, the leaves of which would be for the healing of the nations. I believe that may well be Canada's role..."

"...[Canada] could become a spiritual superpower, showing the rest of the world the way."

214

PREVIOUS FLAGS

THE ST. GEORGE'S CROSS

The St. George's Cross was "the English flag of the 15th century. It was carried by John Cabot, a Venetian sailing under English colours, and flown over Canadian soil when he reached the East Coast of Canada in 1497 [and claimed it for God and for England]."[233]

THE FLEUR DE LYS

The Fleure de Lys was "a symbol of French sovereignty in Canada from 1534, when Jacques Cartier landed and claimed the new world for France, until the early 1760s, when Canada was ceded to the United Kingdom. Although a number of French military flags were used in Canada during this period, including the white flag of La Marine Royale after 1674, the Fleur de Lys held a position of some prominence."[234]

ROYAL UNION

"In the early 1760s, the official British flag was the two-crossed jack or the Royal Union flag (known more commonly as the Union Jack). First flown in 1621, the Royal Union flag was used at all British establishments on the North American continent from Newfoundland to the Gulf of Mexico. This flag is often referred to as the flag of Canada's United Empire Loyalists."[235]

ROYAL UNION (II)

"The Royal Union (II) was used following the Act of Union between Great Britain and Ireland in 1801, the diagonal Cross of St. Patrick was incorporated with England's St. George's Cross and Scotland's Cross of St. Andrew. This gave the Royal Union flag its present-day configuration. This flag was used across British North America and in Canada even after Confederation in 1867."[236]

THE RED ENSIGN

"The Red Ensign, a red flag with the Union Jack in the upper corner, was created in 1707 as the flag of the British Merchant Marine. From approximately 1870 to 1904, it was used on land and sea as Canada's flag, with the addition of a shield in the fly bearing the quartered arms of Ontario, Quebec, Nova Scotia and New Brunswick. Although its use on land had never been sanctioned except by public usage, in 1892 the British admiralty approved the use of the Red Ensign for Canadian use at sea. This gave rise to the name the Canadian Red Ensign. As new provinces entered Confederation, or when they received some mark of identification (sometimes taken from their seal), that mark was incorporated into the shield on the Canadian Red Ensign. By the turn of the century, the shield was made up of the coats of arms of the seven provinces then in Confederation. In 1924, this unofficial version of the Canadian Red Ensign was changed by an Order in Council and the composite shield was replaced with the shield from the royal arms of Canada, more commonly known as the Canadian Coat of Arms. At the same time, this new version was approved for use on Canadian government buildings abroad. A similar order in 1945 authorized its use on federal buildings within Canada until a new national flag was adopted."[237]

"...Canada is predominantly a Christian country. Our compassionate social legislation owes its origins to Christianity. Integrity and compassion and concern for the family – virtues which infuse public and private morality in Canada – reflect the importance of underlying Christian morality in Canada. That is symbolized by the cross within

217

the Union Jack. The colour red in the background of the flag symbolizes life and blood — blood shed in the settlement of this country and in wars to preserve basic freedoms, now very much in peril. Blue in the Union Jack and in the crest represents the oceans, lakes and rivers which are so important to Canadians for transportation, fisheries and, in the case of the fresh waters, for drinking water and irrigation. Traditionally, blue symbolizes loyalty and dedication. White suggests purity and honourable intentions. Additionally, white suggests the vast snows of Canada, an Arctic nation. The components of the Union Jack reflect the Christian core of the peoples of the British Isles. The Cross of St. Andrew (the white 'x' on the blue background) is the ancient flag of Scotland. The Cross of St. George (red cross on white background) is an ancient English banner. The red 'x' on the white background is St. Patrick's cross of Ireland."[238]

"Canada is predominantly a Christian country. Our compassionate social legislation owes its origins to Christianity. Integrity and compassion and concern for the family — virtues which infuse public and private morality in Canada — reflect the importance of underlying Christian morality in Canada."

CANADA'S CREST

"Canada's coat of arms adopted a reference to Psalm 72:8."

"Canada's coat of arms, adopted in 1921, stands upon the Latin phrase A Mari Usque Ad Mare, which when translated means from sea to sea, a reference to Psalm 72:8."[239]

"The crest contains three maple leaves with stems joined. The three leaves represent the component peoples of Canada: the natives, the French and English original settlers, and the others, mostly European, who came later. The veins of the leaves are gold, symbolizing wealth — wealth created through unity and passion for this land and hard work. The Maple Leaf, of course, also represents the forests of Canada — a most important contributor to the nation's wealth. These maple leaves also match the anthem <u>The Maple Leaf Forever</u>...The emblems within the crest reflect the origins of our founding peoples. The couchant lion (upper left), emblem of William of Normandy, has been used by the British monarchs since 1066. It represents both the British and French settlers, the latter mostly from France. The red lion rampant (upper right) was the emblem of the Scottish monarchs. From Cape Breton to Glengarry County, Ontario, Scots, many refugees from the Highland clearances, were important early settlers and leaders (like Sir John A. Macdonald) in Canada. The harp (lower left) is a symbol of Ireland — another important source of our founding people. The Fleur de Lys symbolizes the early French settlers of Canada, who brought this as an emblem of a royalist not a republican France."[240]

"The three leaves represent the component peoples of Canada: the natives, the French and English original settlers."

"The veins of the leaves are gold, symbolizing wealth—wealth created through unity and passion for this land and hard work."

220

CHAPTER 6:
•
CANADA'S PARLIAMENTARY BUILDINGS

PAUL FORESTH'S SPEECH AT THE CANADIAN PRAYER BREAKFAST, 1998

"The evolution of our Parliament is a multi-layered story that...is characteristically Christian in its historical stream. The authority of the Canadian Parliament follows in a line from God. The Queen is the one to whom we as Parliamentarians swear our allegiance and derive our operational legal authority. That authority comes to the Queen from God through the Coronation Ceremony, with a Christian prayer, in a Christian church, with a Christian crown, set amid Christian liturgy. Many of our Canadian Parliamentary symbols follow in the Christian context. We have Ministries and Ministers. Historical Christian motifs are carved in our parliamentary buildings. In our Parliament, we see the Peace Tower windows. Above the east window in the tower is inscribed, 'He shall have dominion also from sea to sea' (Psalm 72:8). Above the south window it says, 'Give the king Thy judgments, O God, and Thy righteousness unto the king's son' (Psalm 72:1). The west window has 'Where there is no vision, the people perish' (Proverbs 29:18). Carved on the largest bell of the tower is 'Glory to God in the highest, and on Earth peace and good will to men' (Luke 2:14).

"Above the east window in the tower is inscribed, 'He shall have dominion also from sea to sea' (Ps 72:8)...above the south window it says, 'Give the king Thy judgments, O God, and Thy righteousness unto the king's son (Psalm 72:1)... The west window has 'Where there is no vision the people perish' (Proverbs 29:18)."

> *"Carved in the Speaker's chair among other maxims, is the phrase, 'Laus Deo'—praise to God, to remind us lest we get too puffed up."*

Carved in the Speaker's chair among other maxims, is the phrase, 'Laus Deo' — praise to God, to remind us lest we get too puffed up. The House of Commons foyer has four creatures carved in stone — the bull, the lion and the eagle, taken from both Ezekiel 1:10 and Revelation 4:6,7. There are scriptural carvings in the Cabinet room and the Opposition Boardroom. The Peace Tower Memorial is replete with scriptural references. Therefore in view of our history, of recognizing where we came from as a society, and who we are, we say we need commensurate leadership to meet the challenges of tomorrow. In community after community, we need leaders to come forward to defend what is good, and to find a wisdom that comes from even beyond our own abilities. It follows that leaders who have learned the value of private prayer, have learned the principles of character development, and first the governance of self, to then be prepared to govern others...Here in Ottawa, MP's and Senators informally come together each Wednesday morning for a non-partisan, spiritual time-out, to read a scripture verse, pray for our country and our colleagues, and reflect that there is indeed a spiritual component to meaningful life. In closing, I say on behalf of my colleagues may we not be too proud to pray. Then may we have ears to hear what the Spirit says. May we

> *"Carved on the largest bell of the tower is 'Glory to God in the highest, and on Earth peace, good will to men' (Luke 2:14)."*

allow prayer to help us become better leaders. Through prayer, the Lord works from the inside out. Parliamentarians work from the outside in. Society would take people out of the slums. Christ takes the slums out of people, and then they take themselves out of the

224

"May we not be too proud to pray. Then may we have ears to hear what the Spirit says. May we allow prayer to help us become better leaders."

slums. Governments mold mankind by changing their environment. Christ changes mankind, who then change their environment. Governments try to shape human behavior, but Christ can change human behavior. May we have leadership that knows how to pray."[241]

Left: Ottawa Parliament

Below:
Peace Tower Bell

CHAPTER 7:
•
CANADA'S PARLIAMENTARY PRAYERS

FIRST DAY OF PARLIAMENT
November 7th, 1867

The first order of activity in the house was a prayer.

1877 DEBATES
TO INTRODUCE PRAYER TO
THE HOUSE OF COMMONS

MR. MACDONALD
Motion for Parliamentary Prayer
MP, Toronto
February 12th, 1877

"Mr. Macdonald (Toronto) moved: 'That it be an order of the House that each day, and immediately after the Speaker shall have taken the chair at three o'clock in the afternoon, that the prayers now read daily in the Senate be read in this chamber by such Chaplain as the Speaker may appoint for the purpose, and in his absence by the Clerk of the House.' He said he rose with a great deal of diffidence to bring this matter before this House, a diffidence produced by the very great importance of the subject, and a fear that he should fail in presenting it with that clearness and force which the subject deserved...He had been very careful in the construction of his

"He was not prepared to believe that any member of this House, whatever might be his religious feelings, could be opposed to soliciting the Divine guidance upon their deliberations."

resolution. He could not fancy that what was right in the Senate could be wrong in the Commons. He was not prepared to believe that any member of this House, whatever might be his religious feelings, could be opposed to soliciting the Divine guidance upon their deliberations. He did not forget that the House was composed of Hon. Gentlemen differing in language, in religion, and in race, but neither did he forget that the Hon. Members of this House were all Canadians, and that Canadians were Christians. He could not forget either that there were many in this House and out of this House who regarded it as dishonoring them, that in the deliberations of this House, upon which so much of the happiness and prosperity of this country depends, God was not acknowledged. Moreover, he could not forget that whatever might be the religious opinions of members of this House, there were none of them who ignored the inspiration of God's Word, and that Word said that there are no powers but that are of God and the powers that are ordained of God. The Hon. Member quoted from the journals to show that in 1792 a resolution was passed in the Legislative Council of the Province of Quebec, providing for the prefacing of the proceedings of the House daily with the reading of a prayer by the Chaplain of the House, and in his absence by the Clerk, a form of prayer for the purpose having been drawn up at the request of the House by the Roman Catholic Bishop and the Protestant Rector of the city of Quebec. This prayer was used daily until the union of the Provinces, when the form now used in the Senate was introduced and made use of until 1866, and it was then merely modified sufficiently to meet the change in the circumstances occasioned by Confederation...We lived in times of greater catholicity, when the sounds of the country would demand that in the

"There were none of them who ignored the inspiration of God's Word, and that Word said there are no powers but that are of God and the powers that are ordained of God."

Senate, their deliberations should commence with the invoking of God's blessing. He did not think it was anything for them to be proud of in not having prayers in this house. They were an exception to the legislatures of all civilized countries of which he had any acquaintance. He had been influenced to put this motion upon the paper from being present in the House of Representatives in Baltimore last May, and seeing that the proceedings were opened with prayer...he did say that hundreds of thousands of the people of the Dominion wanted and asked that a prayer be read, and he did not think that in following the precedent of the Imperial Parliament in regard to this matter they could go far astray...he trusted that today they would...discharge this duty which should have been discharged before; a duty to which they owe to themselves, to their children and to the people of Canada, whose representatives they are."[242]

"Thousands of people of the Dominion wanted and asked that a prayer be read...a duty to which they owed to themselves, to their children and to the people of Canada whose representatives they are."

MR. MACKENZIE

"...[M]embers of Parliament had at heart the welfare of the country in which they performed their duties, and that in a higher sense were responsible to the Almighty."

"...[He] said so far as the motion was condemned there could be little question among members present that what was proposed was a Christian duty. While it was not considered necessary to open the deliberations of all bodies with prayer, it was very plain that the Legislature of the country occupied by municipal councils, agricultural associations and corporate bodies, and that members of Parliament had at heart the welfare of the country in which they performed their duties, and that in a higher sense were responsible to the Almighty. He had always held those views."[243]

SIR JOHN A. MACDONALD

"It was quite proper that the blessing of the Almighty should be invoked upon the acts of the Legislature."

"...[S]aid he agreed with the remarks of those who had spoken on the matter. He felt as a body composed of representatives of a Christian country and supposed to be Christians themselves, that it was quite proper that the blessing of the Almighty should be invoked upon the acts of the Legislature...he would advise that a conversation should take place in the House on the matter and that it should be left to a committee to inquire into and see how it could be carried out."[244]

INTERESTING NOTE: DOMINION DAM ON DEVIL LAKE

The next order of business after the motion and brief discussion regarding prayer in the House was "Dominion Dam on Devil Lake."[245/25]

---

[25] I could not resist including this quote. It just seemed way too appropriate that right at the same time that a motion was being put forth for regular prayer in Parliament that a discussion was happening regarding the DOMINION DAM ON DEVIL LAKE! Yes Lord! May your dominion, fortified through the intercession and lives of your people, dam up every work of the Devil in our nation! I think the Holy Spirit put this one in the House Debates for righteous comic relief!

HOUSE OF COMMONS
PROCEEDURE AND PRACTICE
By Robert Marleau and Camille Montpetit

"PRAYERS

"Prior to the doors of the Chamber being opened to the public at the beginning of each sitting in the House, the Speaker takes the Chair and proceeds to read the prayer."

Prior to the doors of the Chamber being opened to the public at the beginning of each sitting in the House, the Speaker takes the Chair and proceeds to read the prayer, after it has been determined that a quorum of 20 members including the Speaker is present, and before any business is considered. While the prayer is being read, the Speaker, the Members and the Table Officers all stand. When the prayer is finished, the House pauses for a moment of silence for private thought and reflection. At the end of the moment of silence, the Speaker orders the doors opened and the proceedings of the House then begin. At this point, television coverage of the proceedings commences and the public enters the galleries. Although the practice of reading a prayer at the start of each sitting was not codified in the Standing Orders until 1927, it has been part of the daily proceedings of the House since 1877. At that time, the House charged a committee to consider the desirability of using a form of prayer in the Chamber. In its report, the committee recommended that the proceedings of the House should be opened each day with the reading of a prayer and included therein a suggested form of prayer. In a discussion that immediately followed the adoption of the committee report, it was determined that the prayer would be read prior to the doors of the House being opened, as was the practice of

"When the prayer is finished, the House pauses for a moment of silence for private thought and reflection."

234

the Senate of Canada and the British House of Commons. Much later, suggestions were made to rewrite or reword the prayer in a non-sectarian form and to have the prayer read by a chaplain instead of the Speaker. Recommendations have also been made to change the way the House takes up the prayer. Over the years, many Members have expressed the view that the public should be admitted before the prayer is read. In 1976, the House adopted a motion recommending that the Standing Orders be changed in order to allow the public to enter the galleries before the prayer is read. However, the motion was worded as a recommendation, not as an order, and provided no instruction for implementing the change. For that reason, the Speaker indicated that the practice of reciting the prayer prior to the administration of the public would continue until the Standing Committee on Procedure and Organization considered the matter and report to the House; however no further action was taken on this matter. There have been, nonetheless rare instances when the public has heard the prayer. Until 1994, no major change to the form of prayer was made aside from references to royalty. At that time, the House adopted a report recommending a new form of prayer more reflective of the different religions embraced by Canadians."[246]

PARLIAMENTARY PRAYER 1877-1994

The following prayer was prayed before the opening of every parliamentary session in the House of Commons from 1877 to 1994. It has four main parts.

Part #1 is the opening. It contains powerful words of reverence shown towards the LORD. Part #2 could be categorized as the first intercessory section. It is a prayer to honour Canada's positional mother country at this time in history (Britain) and it is a prayer that the royal family would be saved and filled with the Holy Spirit. Part #3 is a prayer of blessing for all the nations connected with Britain. Lastly, the 4th section of the prayer is the "LORD's Prayer" given to the disciples by Jesus. Here it ends on the line "deliver us from all evil."

It is amazing to meditate on the fact that the heavens over Canada's governmental seat are seeded with these four prayer points! May the fullness of His Kingdom come on Earth as it is in Heaven and may the righteous manifestation of these prayers be released in our generation. May we, the succeeding generation, labour fervently to see the exaltation of Jesus Christ established and maintained over the government of Canada — for His name's sake and glory. Amen and amen!

THE PRAYER

"Our Lord and heavenly Father, high and mighty, King of Kings and Lord of lords, the only Ruler of princes."

"Our Lord and heavenly Father, high and mighty, King of Kings, Lord of lords, the only Ruler of princes, who dost from thy throne behold all the dwellers upon the earth; Most heartily we beseech thee with thy favour to behold our most gracious Sovereign Lady, Queen Elizabeth; and so replenish her with the grace of the Holy Spirit that she may always incline to thy will and walk in thy way: Endue her plenteously with heavenly gifts: grant her in health and wealth long to live; strengthen her that she may vanquish and overcome all her enemies; and finally, after this life, she may attain everlasting joy and felicity; through Jesus Christ our Lord — Amen.

Almighty God, the fountain of all goodness, we humbly beseech thee to bless Elizabeth the Queen Mother, Prince Philip, Duke of Edinburg, Charles, Prince of Wales, and all the Royal Family: Endue them with thy Holy Spirit; enrich them with thy Heavenly Grace; prosper them with all happiness; and bring them to thine everlasting Kingdom; through Jesus Christ our Lord — Amen.

Most gracious God, we humbly beseech thee, as for the United Kingdom, Canada and Her Majesty's other Realms and Territories, so especially for Canada, and herein more particularly for the Governor General, the Senate, and the House of Commons, in their legislative capacity at this time assembled; that thou wouldst be pleased to direct and prosper all their consultations, to the advancement of thy glory, the safety, honor, and welfare of our Sovereign and Her Realms and Territories, that all things may be so ordered and settled by their endeavors, upon the best and surest foundations, that peace and happiness, truth and justice, religion and piety, may be established among us for all generations. These, and all other necessaries for them, and for us, we humbly beg in the name, and through the mediation of Jesus Christ, our most blessed Lord and Savior — Amen.

Our Father who art in heaven, Hallowed be thy Name. Thy Kingdom come. Thy will be done on earth as it is in heaven. Give us this day our daily bread; And forgive us our trespasses, as we forgive those who trespass against us. And lead us not into temptation. But deliver us from evil."[247]

"Thy Kingdom come. Thy will be done on earth as it is in heaven... deliver us from evil."

1994-PRESENT

In 1994 another motion was brought forward regarding the parliamentary prayer. Some in Ottawa felt that the traditional prayer no longer reflected the faith of a growing majority of Canadians. Others disagreed with this assessment. What follows are a few quotes from these debates where, in the fight for righteousness, certain Members of Parliament raised their voices in defense of using the name of Jesus Christ in the prayer. In doing this these ones were making a stance in attempts to maintain the prayer as being offered to the God of the Bible and not simply a 'generic' god. After debate a committee was formed to review the prayer. This committee put forth a suggested amendment to original. The amendment was accepted and the new prayer is cited below.

*Question: Who will arise now and reestablish this age old foundation of righteousness? May **we** boldly arise with faith in our hearts and say, "Here am I send me. I will rebuild for your name's sake LORD, only strengthen my hands with Your grace and favour."*

ELSIE WAYNE

February 10th, 1994 House of Commons Debates
MP, Saint John

"Mr. speaker, the tradition of the House dating back to before Confederation is that each day opens with prayer."[248]

PETER ADAMS

June 8th, 1994 House
of Commons Debates
MP, Peterborough

"Mr. speaker, I have a petition from residents of the city and county of Peterborough. The petitioners state: Whereas the name of our Lord, Jesus Christ, in the Lord's Prayer has been included in the historic parliamentary prayer of the House of Commons since 1867; and whereas Canada was founded and built on the principles of Christianity and the large majority of Canadians profess the Christian faith; therefore, the petitioners call on the House of Commons to close the parliamentary prayer with the words: 'Through Jesus Christ our Lord, Amen.'; and reinstate the Lord's Prayer at the conclusion of the opening prayer."[249]

"Whereas Canada was founded and built on the principles of Christianity and the large majority of Canadians profess the Christian faith; therefore, the petitioners call on the House of Commons to close the parliamentary prayer with the words: 'Through Jesus Christ our Lord, Amen.' "

DON BOUDRIA
MP

"There's a crucifix on top of the Speaker's Chair, so let us not pretend (there isn't)."

"...[He explained] that the House and Parliament are steeped in religious symbols and insisting that a prayer is essential. The Constitution has a reference to God in it. There's a crucifix on top of the Speaker's Chair, so let us not pretend (there isn't). We cannot impose a state religion, or one's religious point of view, nor should we. That's quite true, but that doesn't mean there shouldn't be a prayer in Parliament. I think anyone making that argument would really be stretching it."[250]

THE PRAYER AS OF 1994

"Guide us in our deliberations as members of Parliament...Grant us wisdom, knowledge and understanding to preserve the blessing of this country for the benefit of all to make good laws and wise decisions."

This prayer was suggested by the sixth report of the Standing Committee on Procedure and House Affairs regarding the House prayer: "Almighty God, we give thanks for the great blessings which have been bestowed on Canada and its citizens, including the gift of freedom, opportunity and peace that we enjoy. We pray for our Sovereign Queen Elizabeth, and the Governor General. Guide us in our deliberation as members of Parliament and strengthen us in our awareness of our duties and responsibilities as members. Grant us wisdom, knowledge and understanding to preserve the blessing of this country for the benefit of all and to make good laws and wise decisions. Amen."[251]

Following this prayer is a moment of silence for prayer and private reflection and meditation.

CHAPTER 8
•
ONE NATION
ONE PEOPLE:
A Vision of Unity
Between French
and English Canada

The purpose of this section is to look at the convictions, and stances, of Canadian leaders regarding one of our most difficult national issues: relational tension between French and English speaking Canada. Many of the words quoted in this section reflect a fight in the heart of Canadian leaders to see a genuine national unity both established and preserved in Canada. This desire is an echo of what our first Prime Minister, John A. Macdonald, said when he declared, regarding French and English speaking Canada, "It's God and nature who have made the two Canadas one let no factious men be allowed to put them asunder."[26 / 252] As a generation may we also arise with a fight in our spirits declaring, as Mathew 19:6 does, "What God has joined together, let not man separate."

---

[26] See articles in Chapter 3, page 174 & 175, from the Saint John New Brunswick Morning News, July 3rd, 1867 ("New Dominion Holiday") and The New Brunswick Reporter, June 28th, 1867.

SIR JOHN A. MACDONALD (1815-1891)

Laywer
Founding Father
Canada's First Prime Minister

*"We are to be united
in Holy Matrimony
on 1st July."*

"...[O]n May 22nd a royal proclamation announced that the union of British North America was to come into effect... 'So you see,' he wrote off to Fisher of New Brunswick, 'we are to be united in Holy Matrimony on 1st July.' "[253]

*"Its God and nature
who have made the
two Canadas one let
no factious men
be allowed to put
them asunder."*

"If I had influence over the minds of the people of Canada, any power over their intellect, I would leave them with this legacy: Whatever you do adhere to the union. We have a great nation and shall become one of the greatest in the universe if we preserve it; we shall sink into insignificance and adversity if we suffer it to be broken. It's God and nature who have made the two Canadas one let no factious men be allowed to put them asunder."[254]

247

SIR WILFRED LAURIER

"The governing motive of my life has been to harmonize the diverse elements which compose our country."[255]

LOUIS S. ST. LAURENT
Prime Minister from 1946-1948

"Our nation in its origin is a union of two great races that have joined."

"...Our nation in its origin is a union of two great races that have joined their talents without merging their identities...We have a common pride in being Canadians...We feel that our nation can hold its head high among the nations of the world."[256]

"The talents and the energies of our people are those of free men who work together for the benefit of all...Together, we shall strive, under God's guidance, and with confidence in our future, to build a greater and a better land."[257]

"Together, we shall strive, under God's guidance, and with confidence in our future, to build a greater and a better land."

LESTER B. PEARSON
CAMPAIGN SPEECH (1963)

"We need a united Canada. A unity in diversity."

"...[W]e need a united Canada. A unity in diversity."[258]

"The government that I lead...will do its utmost to reach equality between the two partners...[English and French Canadians] must also come together and know each other better."[259]

"...I also believe that the [difficulties] will enable us to come closer together and understand each other more than ever...we need each other...we are inseparable."[260]

"...[G]enuine progress is being made from one generation to the next...the Canadian nation is a combination of these two peoples who founded and made our country grow. When the day comes when we will no longer be able to speak of Canadian unity in our country, Canada will have ceased to exist and then our two cultures will be in grave danger."[261]

"The two groups must also come together and know each other better."

"We need each other, we are inseparable."

"Quebec...is the fatherland of people who live in other provinces. It needs the means to remain itself...It is in this spirit of sincere cooperation that Canada must turn towards its future...together we can make the causes of unease disappear."[262]

"Our country has no problem more important to resolve, apart from those of peace and work for the population, than sustaining and

"Canadian nation is a combination of these two peoples who founded and made our country grow. When the day comes when we will no longer be able to speak of Canadian unity in our country, Canada will have ceased to exist."

developing the Canadian Confederation...there can be a Canadian nation, within which the two fundamental cultures can develop fully...This can be achieved; I know it."[263]

"Canada is rich and privileged in more ways than one, but above all because it is the repository and the beneficiary of two great cultures."[264]

PIERRE ELLIOT TRUDEAU

Remarks at the Proclamation Ceremony
April 17, 1982: the Day Canada "Left Home"

"Had this country been founded upon a less noble vision, or had our forefathers surrendered to the difficulties of building this nation, Canada would have been torn apart long ago."

"I speak of a Canada where men and women of aboriginal ancestry, of French and British heritage...demonstrate the will to share this land in peace, in justice, and with mutual respect...a Canada which is proud of, and strengthened by its essential bilingual destiny, a Canada whose people believe in sharing and in mutual support, and not in building regional barriers...The Canadian ideal which we have tried to live, with varying degrees of success and failure for a hundred years, is really an act of defiance against the history of mankind. Had this country been founded upon a less noble vision, or had our forefathers surrendered to the difficulties of building this nation, Canada would have been torn apart long ago."[265]

"We know that justice and generosity can flourish only in an atmosphere of trust."

"We know that justice and generosity can flourish only in an atmosphere of trust...if French-speaking Canadians or native peoples or new Canadians do not feel they will be treated with justice, it is useless to ask them to open their hearts and minds to their fellow Canadians."[266]

"No sharing of powers can be a substitute for the willingness to share the risks."

"The Constitution which is being proclaimed today...recognizes our multicultural character...no Constitution, no Charter of Rights and Freedoms, no sharing of powers can be a substitute for the willingness to share the risks."[267]

"I wish simply that the bringing home of our Constitution marks the end of a long winter, the breaking up of the ice-jams and the beginning of a new spring...what we are celebrating today is not so much the completion of our task, but the renewal of our hope—not so much an ending, but a fresh beginning...It is in that spirit of faith...I now invite you, the Queen of Canada, to give solemn proclamation to our new Constitution."[268]

"I wish simply that the bringing home of our Constitution marks the end of a long winter."

PRIME MINISTER
KIM CAMPBELL (1993)

"...I believe that Canadians have the common sense to see that a better future cannot be built on fragmentation."[269]

PRIME MINISTER BRIAN MULRONEY (1987)

"...We agreed to recognize the distinctiveness Quebec brings to Canada, which includes within it two principal language communities within the Federation...It [Meech Lake] reflects a spirit of partnership...The work of nation-building goes on."[270]

PRIME MINISTER JEAN CHRÉTIEN (1995)
Address To the Nation On The Night Before The Referendum

"The end of Canada would be nothing less than the end of a dream."

"For the first time in my mandate as Prime Minister, I have asked to speak directly to Canadians tonight...To stay or to leave. This is the issue of the referendum...The end of Canada would be nothing less than the end of a dream. The end of a country that has made us the envy of the world. Canada is not just any country. It is unique. It is the best country in the world. Perhaps it is something we have come to take for granted...today it's up to each of us to restate our love for Canada. To say we don't want to lose it. What we have built together in Canada is something very great and very noble. A country whose values of tolerance, understanding, generosity have made us what we are...we work out our problems...Don't let anyone tell you that you cannot be a proud Quebecer and a proud Canadian."[271]

"Today it's up to each of us to restate our love for Canada. To say we don't want to lose it."

253

"Do not lose faith in this country...
continue to tell French Canada how important they are to you."

"It is true Canada is not perfect. But I cannot think of a single place in the world that comes closer."[272]

"We must recognize that Quebec's language, its culture and institutions make it a distinct society...To all Canadians outside Quebec, I say do not lose faith in this country. And continue to show the respect, the openness, the attachment, and ... friendship...to your fellow Canadians in Quebec...Continue to tell them how important they are to you. And how without them, Canada would no longer be Canada. How you want them to remain Canadian and you hope, deeply and profoundly, that they choose Canada on Monday. My friends, we are facing a decisive moment in the history of our country...I am convinced that a strong Quebec in a united Canada remains the best solution for all of us."[273]

"I ask those Quebecers who have not yet made their decision to ask themselves these questions when they vote on Monday:...Do you really want to turn your back on Canada? Does Canada deserve that? Are you really ready to tell the world — the whole world — that people of different languages, different cultures and different backgrounds cannot live together in harmony?...Have you found one reason, one good reason, to destroy Canada? Do you really think it is worth abandoning the country we have built, and which our ancestors have left us? Do you really think it makes any sense — any sense at all — to break up Canada?...I urge you, my fellow Quebecers, to listen to your heart — and to your head. I am confident that Quebec and Canada will emerge strong and united."[274]

"I am confident that Quebec and Canada will emerge strong and united."

254

HER MAJESTY THE QUEEN
Proclamation at Canada's
Confederation Ceremony (1867)

"...We therefore...issue this Royal Proclamation, and we do ordain, declare and command that on and after the first day of July, 1867, the Provinces of Canada, Nova Scotia and New Brunswick shall form and be one Dominion under the name of Canada."[275]

KING GEORGE VI
Address to Canada (1939)

"...There is one example in particular that North America can offer to other parts of the world...English and French have shown in Canada that they can keep their pride and distinctive culture...while yet combining to establish a broader freedom and security than either could have achieved alone."[276]

CD LYRICS

SONG #1:

CONFEDERATION SONG

Written By Faytene Kryskow; Mixed By Allan Yuet; Vocalists: Faytene Kryskow (Faytene is a relative of Calixa Lavallee, the author of the music to O Canada) and David Lafon (David is Louis Riel's descendant) Note: we chose to have Faytene and David lay the vocal tracks for this song because of their heritage tie to Lavallee and Riel who are both "fathers" in the nation. We are re-digging ancient wells and claiming them for our King! Faytene and David also did vocal work on the other songs for this same reason.); Keys, Synth and Bass: Dave Dewald; Drums: Allan Yuet.

Lyrics: (All the lyrics to this song were taken from research in Chapter 3.)

Verse 1: (From the Montréal Gazette, July 1867)

The King of years is crowning
Our land with His glory of love
And the King of Kings
Looks smiling down
From heaven above
And the tongues of many men
Sing a song of praise and thanksgiving
For a union more precious,
More precious, than gold.

Chorus: (From Toronto Globe and Mail, 1867)

I love thee noble Canada
I love thee and I pray that God may shelter thee
And bless our dominion
I love thy rivers broad and free
Where God unveils His majesty and I pray
Bless our dominion

Verse 2: (From Ottawa Citizen, July 1st 1867)

Holy love fill our bowers
Gentle peace imbue the sod
All the future may be ours
But today belongs to God
He has laid our broad foundations
Leaving us to build thereon
Lo we stand among the nations
God our living cornerstone!

Chorus 2: (From the British Colonist, July 1st 1867)

All hail to the day
Bright and glorious day
Joins us forever
Bonds none can sever
With God as our friend
Our rights to defend
We've naught to fear
Our God is near

Verse 3: (From Ottawa Citizen, July 1st 1867)

Hear us then O God
Whom all the Earth shall own
Make this an auspicious hour
Lay for us our cornerstone
Lift Thy hands in blessing
Over us from sea to sea
Pointing to the hopes that lie before us
And the future yet to be

SONG #2: OH CANADA

Written By Faytene Kryskow; Produced, Mixed and Mastered By Brad York (Spitfire Studios, Surrey B.C.); Vocalists: Faytene Kryskow, Miriam Dewar & Lily Schnirzius; Guitar and Percussion: Faytene Kryskow; Flute: Tim Stewart; Drums: Allan Yuet; Bass: Brad York.

Lyrics:

O Canada, O Canada
There is healing in that name
O Canada, O Canada
There's a destiny to claim
O Canada, O Canada
The nations call to you
O Canada, O Canada
To accomplish what you are called to

O Canada, O Canada
Do you hear the Spirit say?
O Canada, O Canada
Return to God this day
O Canada, O Canada
Do you hear the Spirit say?
Cry out for Me this day

He will rule from sea to sea
And from the river to the ends of the earth

He lifts the needy from the ashes
And He will crush the evil one
He'll take pity on the weak
And rescue them from certain death
For precious is their blood in His sight
(Psalm 72)

O Canada
Our home and native land
True patriot love
In all thy sons command
With glowing hearts we see thee rise
The true north strong and free
From far and wide O Canada
We stand on guard for thee

God keep our land
Keep it glorious and free
O Canada, **we stand on guard** *for thee*

He will rule from sea to sea

SONG #3:
MAY I HAVE THIS DANCE?

Written By Faytene Kryskow (written in honour of the La Danse, French-English reconciliation tour, 2003, as a gift from English speaking Canada to French speaking Canada); Produced By Graham Ord; Mixed and Mastered by Spitfire Studios (Surrey, B.C.); Vocalists: Faytene Kryskow, David Lafon & Graham Ord; Guitar: Graham Ord; Drums: Alec Maynard; Violin: Merla Watson; Bass: Stephen Chu; Keys: Tim Stewart.

Lyrics:

Oh Ma Cherie
I have seen you from a distance
Seems I hardly know your name
Ma Cherie, my heart is pounding in me
Could this be destiny?

O Ma Cherie
I know it's been a long and hard winter
Scars and scrapes are showing through
But Ma Cherie
When I lift my eyes to heaven
I see my destiny with you

May I have this dance with you?
I hold out my hands to you
May I have this dance with you?
For the rest of our lives

Oh Ma Cherie
Our King will soon be coming
When He looks across this land
Let Him see
A bride no longer broken
A people hand in hand
The winter is over
And the springtime has come
The cooing of doves is heard
All across this land

END NOTES

Picture Sources:

All book cover and book graphics for *Stand On Guard: A Prophetic Call and Research on the Righteous Foundations of Canada* were created and designed by Faytene Kryskow. http://www.flyhighministries.com.

CHAPTER 1: A VISION FOR THIS LAND:
Visions in the Hearts of Canada's First Explorers, Missionaries & Early Christian Contact With the First Nations

[1] Rev. Barry P. Boucher, *Canada's Spiritual Heritage*, http://www.watchmen.org/gathering/gathering99/reports/canada-history.html. Retrieved December 2004.

[2] Ibid.

[3] Ibid.

[4] Canada: Portraits of the Faith website, http://ca.geocities.com/canadaschristianheritage/index.html. Retrieved February 2004.

[5] Don Gilmore and Pierre Turgeon, *Canada: A People's History, Volume* (2002), p. 23-24.

[6] Ibid., p. 23, 24, and 30.

[7] Sharon Dunkel, Jacques Cartier.

[8] Ibid.

[9] Canada: Portraits of the Faith website, http://ca.geocities.com/canadaschristianheritage/index.html. Retrieved February 2004.

[10] Rev. Ed Hird, Samuel & Helene de Champlain: A 400-year old Canadian Couple.

[11] Sharon Dunkle, Samuel de Champlain: For God and For Country.

[12] Rev. Barry P. Boucher, *Canada's Spiritual Heritage*, http://www.watchmen.org/gathering/gathering99/reports/canada-history.html. Retrieved December 2004.

[13] Sharon Dunkle, Samuel de Champlain: For God and For Country.

[14] Ibid.

[15] Ibid.

[16] Ed Hird, The 400th Anniversary of Samuel de Champlain & Sieur de Monts.

[17] Ibid.

[18] Ibid.

[19] Ibid.

267

[20] Don Gilmore and Pierre Turgeon, *Canada: A People's History, Volume* (2002), p. 74.

[21] Ibid.

[22] Ibid.

[23] Michael Clarke, *Canada: Portraits of the Faith,* (1998), p. 17.

[24] Ibid.

[25] Ibid.

[26] Ibid.

[27] Ibid.

[28] Ibid.

[29] Ibid.

[30] Ibid., p. 21.

[31] Ibid.

[32] Ibid.

[33] Ibid.

[34] Ibid.

[35] Ibid.

[36] Ibid.

[37] Ibid.

[38] Ibid.

[39] Ibid.

[40] Ibid.

[41] Ibid., p. 25.

[42] Ibid.

[43] Ibid.

[44] Ibid.

[45] Ibid.

[46] Don Gilmore and Pierre Turgeon, Canada: *A People's History, Volume* (2002), p. 72.

[47] Ibid.

[48] Michael Clarke, *Canada: Portraits of the Faith,* (1998), p. 25.

[49] Ibid., p. 23.

[50] Don Gilmore and Pierre Turgeon, *Canada: A People's History, Volume* (2002), p. 79.

[51] Michael Clarke, *Canada: Portraits of the Faith,* (1998), p. 27.

[52] Ibid.

[53] Ibid.

[54] Ibid.

[55] Ibid.

[56] Rev. Barry P. Boucher, *Canada's Spiritual Heritage*, http://www.watchmen.org/gathering/gathering99/reports/canada-history.html. Retrieved December 2004.

[57] http://www.mun.ca/rels/native/micmac/mic7.html. Retrieved March 2004.

[58] Ibid.

[59] Ibid.

[60] Ibid.

[61] Ibid.

[62] Ibid.

[63] Ibid.

[64] Ibid.

[65] Ibid.

[66] Rev. Barry P. Boucher, *Canada's Spiritual Heritage*, http://www.watchmen.org/gathering/gathering99/reports/canada-history.html. Retrieved December 2004.

[67] Ibid.

[68] David Mainse, *God Keep Our Land*, (1981), p. 147-148.

[69] Michael Clarke, *Canada: Portraits of the Faith*, (1998), p. 35.

[70] Ibid.

[71] Ibid.

[72] Ibid.

[73] Ibid., p. 37.

[74] Ibid.

[75] Ibid.

[76] Ibid.

[77] Ibid.

[78] Ibid.

[79] Ibid.

[80] Rev. Barry P. Boucher, *Canada's Spiritual Heritage*, http://www.watchmen.org/gathering/gathering99/reports/canada-history.html.

[81] Canada: Portraits of the Faith website, http://ca.geocities.com/canadaschristianheritage/index.html. Retrieved February 2004.

[82] Ibid.

[83] Rev. Barry P. Boucher, *Canada's Spiritual Heritage*, http://www.watchmen.org/gathering/gathering99/reports/canada-history.html. Retrieved December 2004.

[84] Michael Clarke, *Canada: Portraits of the Faith*, (1998), p. 47.

[85] Ibid.

[86] Ibid.

[87] Ibid.

[88] Ibid.

[89] Ibid.

[90] David Mainse, *God Keep Our Land*, (1981), p. 58-59.

[91] Ibid.

[92] Ibid., p. 81.

[93] Ibid.

[94] Ibid., p. 59.

[95] Ibid., p. 72-73.

[96] Ibid.

[97] Ibid., p. 33-34.

[98] Ibid.

[99] Jack and Peggy Kennedy, personal interview, December 2004.

[100] Anne Coleman, Intercessors for Canada Prophetic News.

Chapter 1 Picture Sources (in order of display in chapter):

Vikings
http://digital.library.upenn.edu/women/marshall/country/country-I-1.html.
Retrieved December 2004.

John Cabot
http://www.heritage.nf.ca/exploration/jcabot.html. Retrieved December 2004.

Jacques Cartier
John Gilmary Shea, *The Story of a Great Nation* (New York: Gay Brothers & Company, 1886).

Louis de Buade de Frontenac
http://www.mef.qc.ca/FRONTENAC.htm. Retrieved December 2004.

Samuel de Champlain
Henry Kirke, The first English conquest of Canada: with some account of the earlier settlements in Nova Scotia and Newfoundland, 2nd edition (London: S. Low, Marston & Co., 1908) facing 29.

Sieur de Monts
Sieur de Monts, National Archives of Canada, C-114189, ID #10068.

Jesuits
http://www.integraenv.com/camp/Chemicals.htm. Retrieved September 2004.

Jean de Brébeuf
Archives de la Province de France, 15 rue Raymond Marcheron 92170 Vanves, France.

Marie Guyart de L'Incarnation
http://perso.wanadoo.fr/alain.perron/quebechistoire3.html.
Retrieved September 2004.

Paul de Chomedey de Maisonneuve

http://membres.lycos.fr/equipe34/lettreprologue.htm.
Retrieved September 2004.

Paul de Chomedey de Maisonneuve Kneeling in Prayer

http://www.thehomecoming.ca. Retrieved December 2004.

Ville Marie

http://perso.wanadoo.fr/alain.perron/Villemarie.htm.
Retrieved December 2004.

Cross

http://www.boldts.net/Montréal.shtml. Retrieved September 2004.

Jeanne Mance

http://www.er.uqam.ca/merlin/ak691533/jeannemance.htm.
Retrieved November 2004.

Marguertie Bourgeoys

http://www.er.uqam.ca/nobel/r14310/NDdBS/Rupture.html.
Retrieved December 2004.

David Thompson

http://www.northwestjournal.ca/V1.htm. Retrieved November 2004.

Bishop Flemming

http://www.sistersofmercynf.org/history/. Retrieved September 2004.

Archdeacon Wix

www.lindahings.com/stgeorges/photos/page03.html. Retrieved September 2004.

Micmac Women

National Archives of Canada, ID# 20640.

Micmac Prayer Book

http://www.cci-icc.gc.ca/whats-new/news25/prayer-book_e.shtml.
Retrieved December 2004.

William Case

http://www.albertasource.ca/methodist/Own_Voices/G_McDougall_Religious_Exp.
htm. Retrieved November 2004.

Henry Bird Steinhauer

Glenbow Archives. NA-352-4.

Cree Book

http://www.albertasource.ca/methodist/Timeline.htm. Retrieved December 2004.

Father Albert Lacombe

http://www.ucalgary.ca/applied_history/tutor/calgary/lacombe.html.
Retrieved December 2004.

Father Charles Pandosy

http://royal.okanagan.bc.ca/cgi-bin/view?browse=pandosy.
Retrieved December 2004.

William Duncan

http://www.blessedquietness.com/journal/housechu/duncanak.htm.
Retrieved December 2004.

CHAPTER 2: CANADA'S FOUNDERS:
Quotes from Founding Fathers of Canada and Other Influential Persons of the Dominion

[101] Rev. Barry P. Boucher, *Canada's Spiritual Heritage*,
http://www.watchmen.org/gathering/gathering99/reports/canada-history.html.
Retrieved December 2004.

[102] Michael Clarke, *Canada: Portraits of the Faith,* (1998), p. 60.

[103] Paul Knowles, *Canada: Sharing Our Christian Heritag*e, p. 46.

[104] Toronto Globe and Mail, July 1st 1867.

[105] Roger Armbruster, *Two Views of Government,* p. 27.

[106] Michael Clarke, *Canada: Portraits of the Faith*, (1998), p. 41.

[107] Ibid., p. 45.

[108] Canada: Portraits of the Faith website,
http://ca.geocities.com/canadaschristianheritage/index.html.
Retrieved February 2004.

[109] Michael Clarke, *Canada: Portraits of the Faith*, (1998), p. 45.

[110] Canada: Portraits of the Faith website,
http://ca.geocities.com/canadaschristianheritage/index.html.
Retrieved February 2004.

[111] Ibid.

[112] Ibid.

[113] Anonymous, The Unsung Hero—Sir Sanford Fleming.

[114] Ibid.

[115] Ed Hird, The Passion of Louis Riel.

[116] Ibid.

[117] Ibid.

[118] Ibid.

[119] Ibid.

[120] Ibid.

[121] Ibid.

[122] David Mainse, *God Keep Our Land,* (1981), p. 171.

[123] Michael Clarke, Canada: *Portraits of the Faith*, (1998), p. 55.

[124] Ibid.

[125] Ibid.

[126] Ibid.

[127] Ibid.

[128] Ibid.

[129] Ibid.

[130] Ibid.

[131] Ibid., p. 71.

[132] Ibid.

[133] Ibid.

[134] Ibid.

[135] Ibid.

[136] Ibid.

[137] Ibid.

[138] Ibid., p. 75.

[139] Ibid.

[140] Ibid.

[141] Ibid.

[142] Ibid.

[143] Ibid.

[144] Ibid.

[145] Ibid.

[146] Montréal Gazette, July 5th, 1980.

[147] Ibid.

[148] Ibid.

[149] Michael Clarke, *Canada: Portraits of the Faith*, (1998), p. 95.

[150] Ibid.

[151] Ibid.

[152] Ibid.

[153] Ibid.

[154] Ibid.

[155] Their majesties' visit to Canada, the United States and Newfoundland: a chronological record of the speeches and broadcast addresses delivered by Their Majesties King George VI and Queen Elizabeth during their tour of Canada, the United States and Newfoundland, May 17-June 17, 1939., (1939), p. 31-32.

[156] Michael Clarke, *Canada: Portraits of the Faith*, (1998), p. 101.

[157] Ibid.

[158] Ibid.

[159] Ibid.

[160] Ibid.

[161] Ibid.

[162] Ibid.

[163] Paul Knowles, *Canada: Sharing Our Christian Heritage*, p. 9.

[164] Michael Clarke, Canada: Portraits of the Faith, (1998), p. 107.

[165] Ibid.

[166] Ibid.

[167] Ibid.

[168] Ibid.

[169] Canada: Portraits of the Faith website,
http://ca.geocities.com/canadaschristianheritage/index.html.
Retrieved February 2004.

[170] Rev. Barry P. Boucher, *Canada's Spiritual Heritage*,
http://www.watchmen.org/gathering/gathering99/reports/canada-history.html.
Retrieved December 2004.

[171] Library of Parliament Formation and Document Branch, Speech from the Throne
to open the Third Session of the Thirty-Seventy Parliament of Canada,
http://www.pcobcp.gc.ca/default.asp?Language=E&Page=InformationResources&su
b=sftddt&doc=sftddt2004_1_e.htm

[172] Michael Clarke, *Canada: Portraits of the Faith*, (1998), p. 119.

[173] Ibid.

[174] Ibid.

[175] Ibid.

[176] Ibid.

[177] Ibid.

[178] Ibid.

[179] Rev. Barry P. Boucher, *Canada's Spiritual Heritage*,
http://www.watchmen.org/gathering/gathering99/reports/canada-history.html.
Retrieved December 2004.

Chapter 2 Picture Sources (in order of display in chapter):

Samuel Leonard Tilley

The Honourable Samuel Leonard Tilley, MP, Saint John, N.B., February 1869.
© Public Domain Source: National Archives of Canada/PA-012632.

George Brown

George Brown © Public Domain Source: National Archives of Canada / C-009553.

Confederation Portrait

http://www.canadianlawsite.com/constitutional.htm.
Retrieved September 2004.

Confederation Stamp

National Archives of Canada, POS-201.

Fathers of Confederation Photo, Charlottetown
Library and Archives of Canada, C-000733.

Bishop John Strachan
http://www.rbebout.com/queen/libtrin/2pgarr.htm.
Retrieved September 2004.

Egerton Ryerson
http://freepages.genealogy.rootsweb.com/~methodists/groups.htm.
Retrieved September 2004.

Sir Sanford Flemming
"Sandford Fleming (C.M.G.) Ottawa, Ontario. Jan. 1895." Topley, William James.
National Archives of Canada, PA-027407.

Louis Riel
http://www.shsb.mb.ca/Riel/indexenglish.htm.
Retrieved December 2004.

William Howland
http://www.hpedsb.on.ca/smood/fathers/howland.htm.
Retrieved December 2004.

Oliver Mowat
Notman & Fraser / National Archives of Canada / PA-028631.

Timothy Eaton
http://www.laurentian.ca/history/cyberhisto/Grands%20personnages/Eaton1.htm.
Retrieved December 2004.

Robert Stanley Weir
http://www.townshipsheritage.com/FR/Rep/General/canada.html.
Retrieved September 2004.

Nellie McClung
http://www.ucalgary.ca/applied_history/tutor/calgary/mcclung.html.
Retrieved December 2004.

King George VI
http://www.homestead.com/mstecker/brmonport2.html.
Retrieved November 2004.

Agnes MacPhail
http://www.somebuddy.ca/goodwomen/mostwanted/.
Retrieved December 2004.

George P. Vanier
http://www.gg.ca/rideauhall/rm-rece-02_e.asp. Portrait of Georges P. Vanier.
Artist: Charles Fraser Comfort Production: Canada, 1967. Acquisition:
Commissioned by the Government of Canada, date of presentation unknown.
Retrieved November 2004.

Pauline Vanier
http://www.collectionscanada.ca/05/0509/050950/05095005_e.html.
Retrieved December 2004.
Throne
Photo Source: Faytene Kryskow
Ernest Manning
National Archives of Canada/C-87204.
Tagak Curley
Tagak Curley © National Aboriginal Achievement Foundation Reproduced with the
permission of the National Aboriginal Achievement Foundation
Source: website of National Aboriginal Achievement Foundation.

CHAPTER 3:
IN CANADA'S NEWSPAPERS

[180] H. K. C., The New Nation, Montréal Daily, July 2nd, 1867.

[181] John Read, Dominion Day, The Gazette Montréal, July 1st, 1867.

[182] Anonymous, Dominion Day, The Gazette Montréal, July 2nd, 1867.

[183] T. H. Grant, To the Free and Independent Electors of the Country of Megantic, The Quebecer, July 4th, 1867.

[184] Anonymous, Dominion Day, The Montréal Daily, July 2nd, 1867.

[185] George Brown, Confederation Day, The Dominion of Canada, Historical Notes, July 1st, 1867.

[186] Charles Sangster, The New Dominion, The Ottawa Citizen, July 1st 1867.

[187] Edward Heartly Dewart, Canada—A Confederation Ode, The Daily Globe, July, 1867.

[188] Anonymous ("By our own Reporters"), New Dominion Holiday, July 3rd, 1867.

[189] Ibid.

[190] Anonymous, Untitled, The New Brunswick Reporter, June 28th, 1867.

[191] Ibid.

[192] Anonymous, Untitled, The New Brunswick Morning News, July 1st, 1867.

[193] Anonymous, The New Dominion, The New Brunswick Reporter, July 5th, 1867.

[194] Ibid.

[195] Ibid.

[196] Edward Willis, Organization Complete, The Morning News, Saint John, New Brunswick, July 3rd, 1867.

[197] Ibid.

[198] Melville, The Nation's Birthday, The Saint John New Brunswick Morning News, July 1st, 1867.

[199] Anonymous, <u>Untitled</u>, The Newfoundlander Newspaper, July 2nd, 1867.

[200] Ibid.

[201] Ibid.

[202] Ibid.

[203] Anonymous, <u>The North American Confederation</u>, The Courier, July 3rd, 1867.

[204] Anonymous, <u>The Birth of the New Dominion</u>, The British Colonist, June 29th, 1867.

[205] Anonymous, <u>Tuesday Morning, July 2</u>, The Halifax Colonist, July 2nd, 1867.

[206] Phoebe Cary, <u>What God Hath Joined</u>, Acadian Recorder, July 6th, 1867.

[207] Anonymous, <u>National Day</u>, The Halifax Evening Reporter, June 29th, 1867.

[208] Ibid.

[209] Ibid.

[210] Ibid.

[211] Joseph C. Crosskill, <u>Great Union Demonstration—Grand Triumph of British Sentiment—Union Proclamation</u>, The Halifax Reporter, July 2nd, 1867.

[212] Anonymous, <u>Untitled</u>, The Halifax Citizen, July 13th, 1867.

[213] Anonymous, <u>Opening of Parliament</u>, The Daily Globe, November 7th, 1867.

[214] Anonymous, <u>Newfoundland</u>, Halifax Morning Chronicle, July 1st, 1867.

[215] Anonymous, <u>The Harvest</u>, The Quebec Daily News, July 4th, 1867.

CHAPTER 4:
CANADA'S SONG

[216] Library and Archives of Canada, Music Division, Vertical File "O Canada" – B versions, editions arrangements.

[217] Ibid.

[218] Ibid.

[219] Ibid.

[220] Roger Armbruster, *Two Views of Government*, p. 27.

[221] Library and Archives of Canada, Music Division, Vertical File "O Canada" – B versions, editions arrangements.

[222] Ibid.

[223] Helmut Kallmann, <u>The Acceptance of O Canada</u>, The Canadian Composer, April, 1966.

[224] Library and Archives of Canada, Music Division, Vertical File "O Canada" – B versions, editions arrangements.

[225] Ibid.

[226] Ibid.

[227] Ibid.

Chapter 4 Picture Sources (in order of display in chapter):

Sheet Music to O Canada
http://ineb.org Retrieved March 2004.

CHAPTER 5:
IN CANADA'S NAME, FLAG & CREST

[228] http://www.canoe.ca/Canadiana/canname.html, Retrieved March 2004.

[229] Michael Clarke, *Canada: Portraits of the Faith*, (1998), p. 60.

[230] http://www.canadianheritage.gc.ca/progs/cpsc-ccsp/sc-cs/df5_e.cfm. Retrieved March 2004.

[231] http://www.collectionscanada.ca/primeministers/h4-4028-e.html, Retrieved March 2004.

[232] David Mainse, *God Keep Our Land*, p. 10.

[233] http://www.collectionscanada.ca/primeministers/h4-4028-e.html, Retrieved March 2004.

[234] Ibid.

[235] Ibid.

[236] Ibid.

[237] Ibid.

[238] Source unknown.

[239] Canada, Portraits of the Faith website, http://ca.geocities.com/canadaschristianheritage/index.html. Retrieved February 2004.

[240] http://www.canadianheritage.gc.ca/progs/cpsc-ccsp/sc-cs/df5_e.cfm. Retrieved March 2004.

Chapter 5 Picture Sources (in order of display in chapter):

Lester B. Pearson
National Archives of Canada PA-126393.

The Flags (all)
http://www.canadianheritage.gc.ca/progs/cpsc-ccsp/sc-cs/df5_e.cfm. Retrieved March, 2004.

The Crest
http://members.shaw.ca/len92/tests.htm. Retrieved December 2004.

CHAPTER 6:
CANADA'S PARLIAMENTARY BUILDINGS:
Paul Foresth's Speech at the Canadian Prayer Breakfast, 1998

[241] Roger Armbruster, *Two Views of Government*, p. 25.

Chapter 6 Picture Sources (in order of display in chapter):

The Parliament
http://www.liberal.parl.gc.ca/welcome_fr.htm. Retrieved December 2004.
The Peace Bell
http://www.nationalwarmemorial.govt.nz/caril-lon.html. Retrieved December 2004.

CHAPTER 7:
CANADA'S PARLIAMENTARY PRAYERS

[242] Commons Debates, February 12th, 1877
[243] Ibid.
[244] Ibid.
[245] Ibid.
[246] Robert Marleau and Camille Montpetit, House of Commons Procedures and Practice, (2000), p. 357-360.
[247] Ibid.
[248] Parliamentary Debates, February 10th, 1994
[249] Ibid., June 8th, 1994.
[250] The Hill Times, February 17th, 1994.
[251] Parliamentary Debates, February 18th, 1994.

Chapter 7 Picture Sources (in order of display in chapter):

Elsie Wayne
http://www.freedominion.ca/phpBB/viewtopic.php.
Retrieved September 2004.
Don Boudria
http://www.pwgsc.gc.ca/comm/business/text/archives/2002/spring2002/article001-e.html. Retrieved September 2004.

CHAPTER 8:
ONE NATION-ONE PEOPLE

[252]http://www.shield.watchmen.ca, Shield and Cluster Forum. Retrieved December 2004.

[253]Donald Creighton, *John A. Macdonald: The Young Politician*, p. 466.

[254] http://www.shield.watchmen.ca, Shield and Cluster Forum. Retrieved December 2004.

[255] http://www.collectionscanada.ca/primeministers/h4-4022-e.html. Retrieved March 2004.

[256] Ibid., h4-4031-e.html.

[257] Ibid.

[258] Ibid., h4-4030-e.html.

[259] Ibid.

[260] Ibid.

[261] Ibid.

[262] Ibid.

[263] Ibid.

[264] Ibid.

[265] Ibid., h 4-4024-e.html.

[266] Ibid.

[267] Ibid.

[268] Ibid.

[269] Ibid., h 4-4033-e.html.

[270] Ibid., h 4-4022-e.html.

[271] Ibid., h 4-4011-e.html.

[272] Ibid.

[273] Ibid.

[274] Ibid.

[275] Anonymous, The Queen's Proclamation, St. John's Daily, June 5th, 1867.

[276] Their majesties' visit to Canada, the United States and Newfoundland: a chronological record of the speeches and broadcast addresses delivered by Their Majesties King George VI and Queen Elizabeth during their tour of Canada, the United States and Newfoundland, May 17-June 17, 1939., (1939), p. 31-32.

Chapter 8 Picture Sources (in order of display in chapter):

Sir John A. Macdonald

Sir John A. Macdonald © Public Domain Credit: National Archives of Canada/C-006513

Louis S. St. Laurent

http://www.dfait-maeci.gc.ca/department/history/depthistory5a-en.asp. Retrieved November 2004.

Pierre Trudeau

http://gauntlet.ucalga`ry.ca/story/1069. Retrieved September 2004.

BIBLIOGRAPHY

Anonymous, Dominion Day, (The Gazette Montréal, Montréal, Quebec, July 1st, 1867).

Anonymous, Dominion Day, (The Montréal Daily, Montréal, Quebec, July 2nd, 1867).

Anonymous, National Day, (The Halifax Evening Reporter, Halifax, Nova Scotia, June 29th, 1867).

Anonymous, Newfoundland, (Halifax Morning Chronicle, Halifax, Nova Scotia, July 1st, 1867).

Anonymous, Opening of Parliament, (The Daily Globe, Toronto, Ontario, November 7th, 1867).

Anonymous, The Birth of the New Dominion, (The British Colonist, Halifax, Nova Scotia, June 29th, 1867).

Anonymous, The Harvest, (The Quebec Daily News, Montréal, Quebec, July 4th, 1867).

Anonymous, The New Dominion, (The New Brunswick Reporter, New Brunswick July 5th, 1867).

Anonymous, The North American Confederation, (The Courier, St. John's Newfoundland, July 3rd, 1867).

Anonymous, *Their majesties' visit to Canada, the United States and Newfoundland: a chronological record of the speeches and broadcast addresses delivered by Their Majesties King George VI and Queen Elizabeth during their tour of Canada, the United States and Newfoundland, May 17-June 17, 1939*, (London, Macmillan, 1939).

Anonymous, The Unsung Hero—Sir Sanford Flemming, (The Providence Foundation of Canada).

Anonymous, Tuesday Morning, July 2, (The Halifax Colonist, Halifax, Nova Scotia, July 2nd, 1867).

Anonymous, Untitled, (The Halifax Citizen, Halifax, Nova Scotia, July 13th, 1867).

Anonymous, Untitled, (The New Brunswick Morning News, New Brunswick, July 1st, 1867).

Anonymous, Untitled, (The New Brunswick Reporter, New Brunswick, June 28th, 1867).

Anonymous, Untitled, (The Newfoundlander Newspaper, Newfoundland, July 2nd, 1867).

Anonymous, July-August 1991 Newsletter, (The Providence Foundation of Canada).

Armbruster, Roger, *Two Views of Government,* (Niverville, independent publication).

Boucher, Rev. Barry P., *Canada's Spiritual Heritage,* http://www.watchmen.org/gathering/gathering99/reports/canada-history.html. Retrieved December 2004.

Brown, George Confederation Day, The Dominion of Canada, Historical Notes, (Toronto Globe & Mail, Vol. XXIV, No. 156, July 1st, 1867).

C., H. K., The New Nation, (Montréal Daily Witness Gazette, Montréal, Quebec, July 2nd, 1867).

Collard, Andrew, Montréaler Wrote O Canada, (Montréal Gazette, Montréal, Quebec, July 5th, 1980).

Canada. Parliament. House of Commons. – House of Commons Debates : official report. – 3rd Parliament, 4th Session. - Ottawa : Queen's Printer for Canada, 1877.

Canada. Parliament. House of Commons. – House of Commons Debates : official report. – 35th Parliament, 1st Session. - Ottawa : Queen's Printer for Canada, 1994.

Cary, Phoebe What God Hath Joined, (Acadian Recorder, July 6th, 1867).

Clarke, Michael, *Canada: Portraits of Faith,* (Chilliwack, BC, Real to Real, 1998).

Coleman, Anne, Canada! Our Constitution and Calling *Intercessors for Canada Prophetic News Spring, 1992.*

Creighton, Donald, *John A. Macdonald: The Young Politician,* (Toronto, The MacMillian Company of Canada Limited, 1952).

Crosskill, Joseph C., Great Union Demonstration—Grand Triumph of British Sentiment—Union Proclamation, (The Halifax Reporter, Halifax, Nova Scotia, July 2nd, 1867).

Dewart, Edward Heartly, Canada—A Confederation Ode, (The Daily Globe, July, 1867).

Dunkel, Sharon, Samuel de Champlain: For God and For Country, (The Providence Foundation of Canada).

Dunkel, Sharon, Jacques Cartier, (The Providence Foundation of Canada).

Gilmore, Don and Pierre Turgeon, *Canada: A People's History, Volume 1* (Toronto, Ontario, McLelland & Stewart, The Canadian Publishers, 2002).

Grant, T. H., To the Free and Independent Electors of the Country of Megantic, (The Quebecer, July 4th, 1867).

Hird, Ed, Article: The 400th Anniversary of Samuel de Champlain and Sieur de Monts (Vancouver, independent publication, 2003).

Hird, Ed, Article: The Passion of Louis Riel, (North Vancouver, Deep Cover Crier, 2004).

Kallmann, Helmut, The Acceptance of O Canada, The Canadian Composer, April 1966, p.18-19.

Kennedy, Jack and Peggy, personal interview, December 2004.

Knowles, Paul, *Canada, Sharing Our Christian Heritage,* (Toronto, Ontario, Mainroads Productions Inc. 1982).

Marleau Robert and Camille Montpetit, *House of Commons Procedure and Practice,* (Montréal-Toronto, McGraw-Hill, House of Commons).

Mainse, David, *God Keep Our Land*, (Toronto, Ontario, Mainroads Productions Inc. 1981).

Melville, The Nation's Birthday, (The Saint John New Brunswick Morning News, Saint John, New Brunswick, July 1st, 1867).

"O Canada" – B versions, editions, arrangements., Library Archives of Canada, Music Division, Vertical File.

Read, John, Dominion Day, (The Gazette Montréal, Montréal, Quebec, July 1st, 1867).

Sangster, Charles, The New Dominion, (The Ottawa Citizen, Ottawa, Ontario, July 1st 1867).

The Hill Times, *February 17th, 1994,* The Thorny Area of Religion.

The Holy Bible, New King James Version, Copyright 1982 by Thomas Nelson, Inc. Used by permission. All rights reserved.

Willis, Edward, Organization Complete, (The Morning News, Saint John, New Brunswick, July 3rd, 1867).

INDEX

Hudson Bay Company, 106-107, 112, 132.

Huguenots, 79-80, 95.

Huron, 80-84, 209.

Intercessors, 56-57.

Intimidation, 49-50.

Inuit, 40, 71, 157.

Iroquois, 80, 83-84, 87, 209.

Jacobs, Cindy, 55.

Jehu, 56.

Jesuits, 80-87.

Jezebel, 56.

Josiah, 27, 54-55.

l'Incarnation, Marie Guyart de, 46, 84-87.

LaCombe, Father Albert, 109-110.

Laurier, Sir Wilfred, 248.

Literature, 47, 123, 145-146.

Maple Leaf, 212-214, 217. 220.

McClean, Rev. Elwood, 110.

McClung, Nellie, 47, 145-146.

McCulloh, Mercy E. Powell, 200.

Macdonald, Sir John A., 122, 132, 210, 220, 233, 245, 247.

MacDougall, George, 108.

MacPhail, Agnes, 47, 149-150.

Mainse, David, 110, 133, 214.

Maisonneuve, Paul de Chomedey, 47, 88-91, 114.

Mance, Jeanne, 47, 92.

Manitoba (birth of), 131-132.

Manning, Ernest, 155-156.

Martyrdom, 80-84, 199.

May I Have This Dance (song), 263.

Media, 46-47, 53, 123, 155-156.

Methodist, 99-103, 105-107, 115, 127, 128, 140-142.

Métis, 131-133.

Micmac, 95-96.

Missionaries, 67-116.

THANKS

Special thanks to...

...**Father, Son & Holy Spirit**:
~I love you. You do all things well.

...**David Demian, Patricia King,
Alistair Petrie, Peg Byars, Wesley and Stacey Campbell,
Donna Bromley & Sara Maynard**:
*~You have put more breath beneath my wings than you know. Thank
you for stopping for me. You all have been a refuge of grace for me
at pivotal moments. **I honour you before the nation.** I love you and
thank God for you. I pray this publication makes you smile with
zeal and delight, and, that it adds holy fuel to your fire for Canada!*

...my **supporters, Church** & faithful **intercessors** (especially!):
*~Each life that this book touches will be credited to your heavenly
account! Thank you for standing with me and freeing me to do what
I love and am made for.*

...a few of my best comrades in the Spirit,
David Lafon and Kirk & Cheryl Smith:
*~You are "men of might" and trusted friends in battle.
Thank you for guarding my life in this past season.
United we stand — for HIM. And by the way, this nation
belongs to Jesus, want to play capture the flag with me?
Also, I am looking forward to your books!*

...**Colleen Stewart, Darlene Ochotta, Jeff Pelton,
Chris Wright and Steven Court**:
*~Thanks for watching my grammatical & referencing back.
You are woenderful — kidding! You are **wonderful**.*

Last, Not Least...
*Another book for the coffee table **Mom and Dad!***
~Thanks just for being so awesome and engaged.
I also honour you before the nation – you are amazing.
This book has your name on it, I pray it blesses your hearts.

299

OTHER RESOURCES BY

SIGNATURE:
SONGS OF EXTREME INTIMACY

*Hot off the press! Signature is a compilation of Faytene's favorite personal worship compositions. The subtitle says it all! We believe this CD will draw you into **a deep place of intimacy** with Jesus — and we pray it will make you want to stay. Most of the CD is what we would call a "soaker." It is fresh and inspired. Faytene was blessed to be accompanied by some of the best Christian musicians in the Vancouver area for this recording. Accompanying artists include: Tracy Rahn (vocals), Kathleen Nisbet (violin) Eran Vooys (drums), Peter Davyduck (bass), Caleb Chiu (vocals), Brian Thomas (keys, flute and guitar)...and others! May it take you into a deep, deep, place with HIM.*
Cost: $20.00 *(Price subject to change.* See www.flyhighministries.com *for details.)*

KING OF JUSTICE:
SONGS OF A MISSIONARY

*This CD is a compilation of unique songs written by Faytene, mostly while on the 3rd world missions field (Liberia, W. Africa). The CD includes songs that are intercessory, chronicles of missions experiences with the poor, declarations of faith, scriptures and more. There is a ton of **variety**! The one thing all the tracks have in common is that they come from a heart which cries out: **"The bound must be released!, the wounded healed!, the poor assisted!, the lost found!** — all in the name of the King of Justice: Jesus Christ."** Many have testified of how it has moved them to both tears and prayer. It is a CD of the heart — His heart for the suffering. Cost: $15.00 (Price subject to change. See www.flyhighministries.com for details.)*

To order these and other resources by Faytene or for information on her ministry visit www.flyhighministries.com or e-mail fkryskow@yahoo.ca.

STAND ON GUARD:
MUSICAL CD COMPANION TO THE BOOK

As a companion to the book "Stand On Guard: A Prophetic Call & Research on the Righteous Foundations of Canada" Faytene recorded a 3 track musical CD. These songs were all written in times of prayer for the nation and as the Lord stirred a deepening love for the nation in her heart. **As you listen to this short CD we believe a Godly zeal for Canada and for the LORD'S Kingdom will be imparted.** *The CD serves as a powerful musical meditation in conjunction with the message of the book. (Songs Include: "Confederation Song" (taken from the research), "Oh Canada" (a call to the nation to arise into destiny) and "May I Have This Dance?" (a song in honour of the journey of healing the LORD has been doing between French and English speaking Canada). See the Preface and pages 259-263 for the lyrics and a deeper explanation of the heart of these songs. Contributing artists to the music include: Graham Ord (production, guitar and vocals), Tim Stewart (flute and keys), Eran Vooys (drums), Merla Watson (violin), David Lafon (Louis Riels' descendant; vocals) Stephen Chu (bass), Allan Yuet (production and drums), Dave Dewald (keys and bass) and Bradly York (production and guitar).*

Book Alone: $20.00
CD Alone: $8.00
Book & CD together: $25.00

(Prices are subject to change. See www.flyhighministries.com for details.)

WANTED! CANADIAN HEROES
REWARD: A NATION

This CD is not for the faint hearted--it is for the next generation of Canadian revolutionaries! Be prepared to be stirred by the Spirit of God to be one of those in HIS army who will rise up in this hour to reclaim the destiny of HIS DOMINION (Canada).

Musical Description: *Hot beats to Faytene preaching the message of STAND ON GUARD and Tracy Rahn (of the Wildings) going off!! This CD has been an instant hit with the youth and techno lovers especially. (Length: 64 min 40 sec)*

Cost: *$20.00 (Price subject to change. See www.flyhighministries.com for details)*

VANCOUVER:
NOTES FOR INFORMED INTERCESSION

*This compilation of **strategic research** is a must read for anyone wanting to pray effectively for Vancouver, Canada. It is also **an excellent model** for those seeking to do similar research in their own community. The notes include information on everything from First Nation's history and Vancouver's Founding Fathers to recent city statistics. You will find it eye opening, hearty and useful. Note: this is a draft of detailed notes with photos maps and more, this is not an edited publication.*

Cost: $20.00 *(Price subject to change. See* www.flyhighministries.com *for details.)*

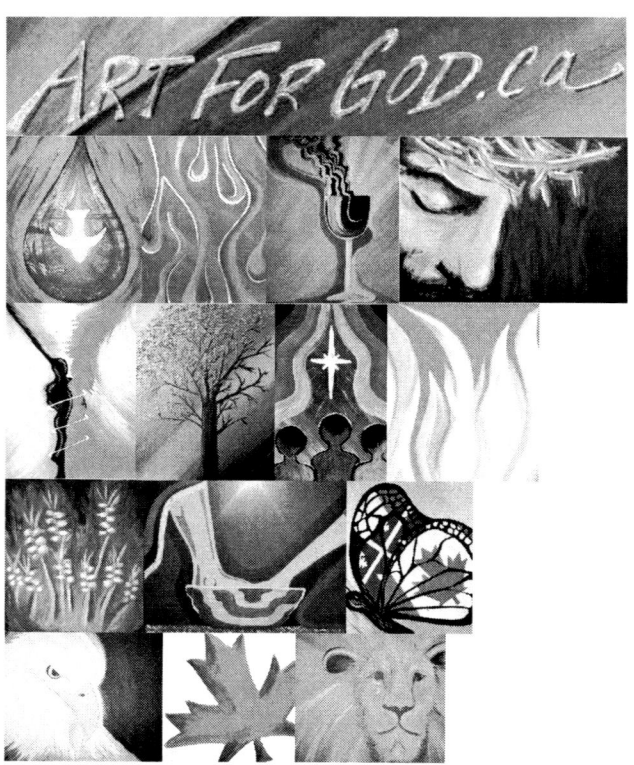

View art by Faytene Kryskow at www.artforgod.ca.

302

OTHER BOOKS BY CREDO PRESS

THE SIREN CALL OF A DANGEROUS GOD:
ESSAYS IN EVANGELICAL DIALECTIC.

The inimitable Geoff Ryan spins a stirring sequel to SOWING DRAGONS that provokes both thought and action. Spring Harvest's Gerard Kelly writes the foreword.

PROVERBIAL LEADERSHIP:
ANCIENT WISDOM FOR TOMORROW'S ENDEAVORS.

Wesley Harris and Stephen Court collect all of King Solomon's 'leader proverbs', examine them and simply apply them for your practical benefit.

WESLEY**HARRIS**
STEPHEN**COURT**

To order Credo Press resources visit www.armybarmy.com.

Conclusion:

He will have DOMINION!